Anonymous

Still Another

A book of choice recips by the Ladies Aid Society

Anonymous

Still Another
A book of choice recips by the Ladies Aid Society

ISBN/EAN: 9783337422950

Printed in Europe, USA, Canada, Australia, Japan

Cover: Foto ©Lupo / pixelio.de

More available books at **www.hansebooks.com**

A
Book of Choice Recipes

BY

THE LADIES' AID SOCIETY

OF THE

FIRST CONGREGATIONAL CHURCH.

SECOND EDITION.

"We may live without poetry, music and art;
We may live without conscience, and live without heart;
We may live without friends; we may live without books;
But civilized man cannot live without cooks.
He may live without books,—what is knowledge but grieving?
He may live without hope,—what is hope but deceiving?
He may l've without love,—what is passion but pining?
But where is the man that can live without dining?"

OAKLAND, CALIFORNIA:
TRIBUNE PUBLISHING COMPANY, NOS. 413, 415 AND 417 EIGHTH STREET,
1883.

PREFACE TO FIRST EDITION.

"STILL another!" cries a long-suffering public. True, but take courage! For, this time it is not a "complete manual" to supply "a want long felt." It is only a book of the favorite cooking recipes of those ladies of our Society who have long been recognized as authorities among us in all matters connected with housekeeping. The recipes are, all of them, among the things Tried and Proven. We have published them for the twofold purpose of binding them together into convenient form for reference and adding to the funds of our Society.

Thus we claim no place among the grand compendiums of Housewifery; we have been humble gleaners in the field of culinary art, and we now lay our gathered sheaf at your feet, hoping you may deem it worthy of a place among your household treasures.

PREFACE TO SECOND EDITION.

The very flattering success of the first issue of "STILL ANOTHER" induced the ladies to issue the present revised and improved edition. Much care has been taken to eliminate all errors; many valuable and rare recipes have been added; and the general appearance of the book improved.

We trust our second edition will meet with as cordial a reception at the hands of a generous and considerate public as did our first.

CONTENTS.

Salads—Chicken Salad—Crab Salad—Potato Salad—Tomato Salad—Cream Slaw.. 9-10

Soups—Soup Stock—Mock Turtle or Calf's Head Soup—Cream of Barley Soup—Tomato Soup—Celery Cream—Onion Soup—Corn Soup—Soup in Two Hours—Bean Soup—Clam Chowder—Crab Soup—Delmonico's Receipt for Oyster Stew......... 11-15

Fish—Fish a la Crême—Cusk a la Crême—Fillet of Sole au Gratin—Club House Fish Cakes—Fried Sole—Fried Flounder—Salt Cod... 16-18

Meats—General Directions.................................. 19-20

Vegetables—General Directions............................ 21

Breakfast and Lunch Dishes—Scalloped Potatoes—Stuffed Potatoes—Stuffed Green Peppers—Scalloped Oyster Plant—Dormers—Corn Oysters—Baked Cauliflower—Tomato Macaroni—Baked Tomatoes—Scrapple—Veal and Ham Pressed—Tongue with Jelly—Boned Chicken—Crab—Hot Crab—Deviled Crab Baked—Omelette—Bread Omelette Nice Breakfast Dish—Baked Meat Stew—Veal Meat Loaf—Clam Pie—Clam Fritters—Boiled Beef—Oyster Cakes—Oyster Fricassee—Creamed Oysters—Scalloped Oysters—Fried Oysters—Fricassee Chicken—Beef a la Daube—Beef a la Mode—Chicken Pie—Baked Beans... 22-31

Bread—Rules for Bread—Family Bread—Potato Yeast—Parker House Rolls—Light Rolls—Beaten Biscuit—Soda Biscuit—New Milk Bread—Biscuit for Small Family—Sally Lunn—Muffins—Mush Muffins—Waffles—Pop Overs—Squash Griddle Cakes—Buckwheat Cakes—Corn Cakes—Corn Bread—Brown Bread—Baked Brown Bread—Graham Bread.................... 33-37

Cake—Rules for Cake—Republican Cake—Imperial Cake—Myrtle Cake Pound Cake—Little Pound Cake—New England Election Cake—Corn Starch Cake—Springfield Cream Puffs—Snow Drops—Mountain Cake—Harrison Cake—Fruit Cake—Sunshine Cake—Vanilla Cake—Poor Man's Cake—Ribbon Cake—Marble Cake—Coffee Cake—Dried Apple Cake—Bread Cake—Sponge Cake—White Sponge Cake—Berwick Snow Cake—Angel Cake—Silver and Gold Cake—Company Cake—Boiled Icing—The New Frosting—Filling for Layer Cake—Nut Cake—English Walnut Cake—Cake with Almond Filling—Lemon Cake—Ambrosia Jelly for Cake—Chocolate Cake—Chocolate Eclairs—Cocoanut Cake—Lemon Cake—Orange Cake—Jelly Cake—Jelly Roll—Jelly Fruit Cake—Harlem Jumbles—Nahant Buns—Doughnuts—Crullers—Caraway Cookies—Ginger Crackers—Ginger Bread—Old Fashioned Sugar Ginger Bread—Molasses Ginger Bread—Ginger Cake—Rochester Molasses Cookies............................ 39-51

Light Desserts—Ambrosia—Chocolate Bavarian Cream—Charlotte Russe—Sherbet—Isinglass Blanc Mange—Spanish Cream—Tapioca Cream—Pink Cream—Bananas and Cream—Oranges for Lunch—Strawberry Ice—Peach Custard—Our Favorite Apple Meringue—Ice Cream—Trifle—Macaroon Pudding—Cocoanut and Chocolate Blanc Mange—A Delicious Dessert—Sweet Cream.. 52-58

Pastry and Puddings—Rules for Pastry—Puff Paste—Lemon Pie—Lemon Tarts—Raisin Pie—Transparent Tarts—Cocoanut Tarts—Strawberry Short Cake—Squash Pie—Mince Pie—Cream Pie—Lemon Pudding—Bread Pudding—English Plum Pudding—Snow Pudding—Corn Starch Pudding—Plain Suet Pudding—Omelette Pudding—Batter Pudding—Baked Indian Pudding—Fruit Pudding—Rice Pudding—Coffee Pudding—Sweet Potato Pudding—Carrot Pudding—Queen's Pudding—Snow Pudding—Indian Pudding—Sauces for Puddings—Oyster Sauce for Boiled Chicken—Drawn Butter—Egg Sauce—Cranberry Sauce... 59-67

Confectionery—Almond Bread—Chocolate Creams—Macaroons—Butter Scotch—Caramels—Old Fashioned Molasses Candy—Kisses—Uncooked Cream Candy.. 68-69

Preserved Fruits—Canned Fruits—Fruit Jellies—Currant Jellies—Raspberry and Blackberry Jam—Apple Jelly—Lemon Jelly—Fig Marmalade—Preserved Figs—Spiced Currants—Spiced Blackberries—Spiced Peaches.............................. 70-73

Pickles and Catsups—Pickled Peaches—Ripe Cucumber Pickles—Fig Pickles—Green Tomato Sweet Pickle—Cucumber Pickles—Mixed Pickles—Tomato Hodge Podge—Chow Chow—Picalilli—Grape Catsup—Plum Catsup—Chile Sauce............. 74-77

A Chapter for Dyspeptics—Unleavened Bread—Graham Bread—Graham Gems—White Gems—Beaten Biscuit—Graham Crackers—Rye or Indian Drop Cake—Old Fashioned Johnny Cake—Graham Mush—Cracked Wheat—Hominy—Boiled Rice—Scotch Pudding—Oat Meal Blanc Mange—Indian Pudding—Granula Pudding—Simple Fruit Short Cake—Graham Pie Crust—Corn Soup—Rice Soup—Mutton Toast—Favorite Aphorisms.. 79-83

Drinks—Tea—Coffee—Chocolate—Cocoa—Refreshing Drink for the Sick—Raspberry Acid—Currant Ice Water—Effervescing Fruit Drinks—Beef Extracts—Beef Tea................... 85-87

Miscellaneous—Japanese Cleaning Cream—To Renovate Carpets and Furniture—Celery Salt—A Cure for Asthma—Odds and Ends—Last Words, Etc., Etc............................... 89-90

A Chapter received too late for classification, containing directions for carving, and many valuable recipes............. 115-124

FREUD'S CORSET HOUSE.

"The Corset Emporium of America."

OUR CORSETS
Combine Grace, Comfort and Economy.

Sole Agency for the Best Factories in the World.

742 and 744 MARKET STREET,
SAN FRANCISCO.

OUR Corsets
Are perfect in Fit, Shape and Finish.

Only Depot for the Genuine French Corsets.

10 and 12 Dupont Street,
SAN FRANCISCO.

Wholesale and Retail Catalogues sent FREE to any Address.

For THE MOST STYLISH

MILLINERY

GO TO

AT VERY REASONABLE PRICES.

No. 10 Kearny St., San Francisco.

Wholesale and Retail

CLOAK

— AND —

SUIT

HOUSE,

No. 105 Kearny Street,

Next to White House,   San Francisco.

SALADS.

CHICKEN SALAD.—*Mrs. Israel Knox.*

One boiled chicken, one head lettuce, one head celery, slice with sharp knife, and prepare the following dressing:—

One cup of weak vinegar, one tablespoonful of butter, one teaspoonful salt, one heaping teaspoonful of mustard; one small cup of cream, three eggs. Put the vinegar, butter, and salt in a porcelain saucepan to heat; while it is heating, mix the mustard by gradually adding the cream; then beat the eggs, and add them; then pour the hot mixrure slowly on the cream, etc., stirring all the time; put the whole mixture over the fire, stirring every moment until it *nearly* boils; then strain and put in a cool place.

CHICKEN SALAD NO. 2.—*Mrs. Van Blarcom.*

Cut the meat of a pair of fowls into small dice; add to this meat about two-thirds more of celery sliced very thin; mix in a cup, white pepper, one teaspoonful; mustard, one very small teaspoonful; salt one teaspoonful; Worcestershire sauce, one tablespoonful; vinegar, one-half cupful. Cut an onion in half, and wipe with it the bowl in which you will mix your salad. Add your spices by degrees, tasting from time to time to get it just right. For your mayonnaise, the yolk of an egg, a bottle of oil, a soup plate and a fork. Drop the oil on the yolk of the egg in the plate, stirring it well. When too stiff, add a few drops of vinegar or lemon juice, and go on adding oil till you have as much dressing as is needed. If you are impatient and add the oil too fast, and it "curdles," save your time by beginning over again, with a new yolk, and more patience.

CRAB SALAD.—*Mrs. Dr. Ober.*

Have ready the choicest parts of two head of lettuce in small pieces, and the flesh of two boiled crabs, reserving the oil of the crabs in a small dish. Place in a large soup-plate the yolk of a hard-boiled egg, and rub till smooth. Add the yolks of two raw eggs, one teaspoonful of *freshly mixed* mustard, one teaspoonful of sugar, and a pinch of salt. Commence stirring (using a wooden salad

---

Income of Firemans' Fund Insurance Company, $2,000 per day!

spoon) with the right hand, holding a bottle of salad oil in the left dropping it by degrees, and continually stirring it until you have used about one-fourth bottle of oil, when you should have a thick, smooth mixture. Then stir in a tablespoonful of vinegar, and it will form into a rich, creamy-looking dressing. Now stir in the oil of the crab, and next add the flesh of the crab broken in small pieces. Place lettuce in a salad bowl, and pour dressing over it, lightly mixing with a salad fork. Garnish with hard-boiled egg cut in rings. The lightest scatter of pepper over the whole, and it is ready to serve. This makes enough for six persons.

POTATO SALAD.—*Mrs. Walker.*

Mash fine two boiled potatoes; add one teaspoonful of mustard, one teaspoonful of salt, four teaspoonfuls of sweet oil, three teaspoonfuls of sharp vinegar; add the yolks of two boiled eggs rubbed fine; mix first the egg and potato; and the mustard and salt; gradually mix the oil, stirring all the while; add the vinegar last. The more stirred the better it will be.

POTATO SALAD.—*Mrs. Dyer.*

For a good-sized dish of boiled cold potatoes take the yolks of two hard-boiled eggs, yolk of one raw egg, one-half teaspoonful pepper, one teaspoonful of salt, one tablespoonful of mustard, two tablespoonfuls of vinegar, one-half cup of oil, celery, and onions chopped fine.

TOMATO SALAD.—*Mrs. C. A. Grow.*

Place ripe tomatoes some time before wanting on ice. Just before serving, pare and cut into slices. Arrange on a flat dish with a little mayonnaise dressing on each slice. Garnish with a delicate border of parsley.

CREAM SLAW.—*Mrs. Charles Ames.*

Shave, not chop, cabbage very fine, sprinkle over it a little salt and black pepper; put on the stove to warm a lump of butter the size of a walnut, with a little flour dredged in; when this is melted together stir into it three tablespoonfuls of cream, and let it come to a boil; remove from the stove, then turn in the shaved cabbage and stir thoroughly, and add at the last a beaten egg.

Swiss Confectionery, { Ladies' and Gentlemen's Ice Cream and Coffee Saloon, 416 Twelfth Street. Wm. J. F. Laage, Prop.

SOUPS.

SOUP STOCK.—*Mrs. Israel Knox.*

One good stock is the foundation of all soups.

To a two-bit shin of beef I add what beefsteak and other meat bones I may have, add six quarts of water, cover tightly, and boil gently all day. Strain at night and set away to cool. The next day skim the fat from it and if the stock is not a thick jelly, put it on the stove and boil still longer. This should make three quarts of rich jelly, to which you can add rice, barley, macaroni, vermicelli or vegetables, or whatever you fancy as a flavoring. (The fat I skim from the soup I put on the stove and boil until it is transparent, pour it into a small pan or tin and use it in place of butter or lard for cooking. It is much superior to butter or lard for frying or shortening.)

MOCK TURTLE OR CALF'S-HEAD SOUP.
Mrs. J. K. McLean.

One large calf's head, four pig's feet.

This soup should always be prepared the day before it is to be served up. Lay the head and feet in the bottom of a large pot, and cover with a gallon of water. Let it boil three hours, or until the flesh will easily slip from the bones. Take out the head, leaving in the feet, allow these to boil steadily, while you cut meat from the head. Select enough of the fatty portions which lie in the top of the head and the cheeks to fill a teacup, and set aside to cool. Remove the brains to a saucer, and also set aside. Chop the rest of the meat, with the tongue very fine; season with salt, pepper, powdered marjoram, and thyme, teaspoon of cloves, teaspoon of mace, half as much allspice, a grated nutmeg, and return to the pot. When flesh falls from pig's feet, take out the latter, leaving the meat. Boil all together slowly, without removing cover, for two hours more, then set away till next day. An hour before dinner, set on stock to warm. When it boils strain carefully, drop in the meat which you have reserved, which when cold, should be cut in small squares. Have these all ready as well as the force-meat balls. To prepare these, rub yolks of five hard-boiled eggs to a paste, adding gradually the brains to moisten them, also a little butter and salt. Mix with these two eggs beaten very light, flour your hands, and make this paste into balls about the size of pigeon's eggs; put these into the soup about five minutes before taking from the fire, stir a large tablespoonful of browned flour, rubbed smooth in some cold water, let it boil up, add juice of one lemon. It should not boil more than one-half hour on second day. Serve with sliced lemon.

CREAM OF BARLEY SOUP.—*Mrs. Wheeler.*
GERMAN STYLE.

Soak the barley over night. In the morning pour the water off, add fresh and boil ten minutes. Then cover with bouillon. Put in it one onion and a bouquet. Let it boil slowly two hours; then strain through a sieve, allowing most of the barley to pass through. Place on the stove and boil five minutes. Skim the fat off and add a cup of rich milk or cream. If desired, add the beaten yolks of two eggs.

TOMATO SOUP.—*Mrs. Pliny Bartlett.*

Four good-sized tomatoes, boiled with skins on, in a quart of water. Put in a colander and mash; then put a teaspoonful of soda in the tomatoes. Boil one quart of milk, add butter, pepper and salt, same as for oyster soup. Roll a cracker and put it in the milk, add the two together and serve.

CELERY CREAM.

Take a quart of clear soup stock or the water in which chickens have been boiled; put on the stove half a cup of rice in a pint of rich milk, grating into it the white part and roots of a head of celery. Let the rice and milk cook very slowly at the back of the stove, adding more milk if it gets stiff. Season with salt and a little white pepper. Strain, add it to stock (warmed) and boil together for a few minutes. It should look like rich cream and be strongly flavored with celery. This makes three pints of soup.

ONION SOUP.—*Mrs. Israel Knox.*
A SOUP WITHOUT MEAT, AND DELICIOUS.

Put into a saucepan butter size of a pigeon's egg. Clarified grease,

---

J. Letter, Gentlemen's Furnishing Goods, 1001 Broadway.

or the cakes of fat saved from the top of stock or soup answers as well. When very hot add two or three large onions, sliced thin; stir, and cook them well until they are red; then add a half teacupful of flour; stir this also until it is red, watching it constantly, that it does not burn. Now pour in about a pint of boiling water, and add pepper and salt; mix it well and let it boil for a minute, then pour it into the soup-kettle and place it at the back of the range until almost ready to serve. Add then one and one-half pints or one quart of boiling milk, and two or three well-mashed potatoes. Add to the potatoes a little of the soup at first, then more, until the potatoes are smooth and thin enough to put into the soup-kettle. Stir all well and smoothly together; taste, to see if the soup is properly seasoned with pepper and salt, as it requires plenty. Let it simmer for a few moments.

Put pieces of toasted bread, cut in diamond shape, in the bottom of the tureen, pour over the soup and serve very hot. Or, this soup might be made without potatoes, if more convenient, using more flour and all milk, instead of a little water. However, it is better with the potato addition; or it is much improved by adding stock instead of water; or, if one would chance to have a boiled chicken, the water in which it was boiled might be saved to make this soup.

SOUP IN TWO HOURS.—*Mrs. Van Blarcom.*

Two pounds of lean, juicy beef, three quarts of water, vegetables to your taste. Let the butcher cut the meat into quite small pieces, and the cook chop the vegetables. Simmer well, but do not allow it to boil hard. When ready to serve, strain it and serve as a clear soup, or add sago. Light egg dumplings are very nice in this soup.

CORN SOUP.—Very nice.—*Mrs. R. E. Cole.*

Cut or grate carefully the corn from one dozen ears. Put the cobs into a kettle with one quart of water, and boil twenty minutes. Remove the cobs and add to the water the corn and one quart of milk, and boil for ten minutes. Remove from the fire, season with salt and pepper to taste, and a large piece of butter; stir in two well beaten eggs.

Try Fish & Co's Block Butter, Eighth and Market.

BEAN SOUP.—*Mrs. R. E. Cole.*

One pint of beans boiled until very tender with two quarts of water, strain through a colander, rubbing the beans through, return to the fire and add one quart or more of milk, and let it boil up once, add salt, pepper, and butter; it requires a good deal of seasoning, but is well worth the material.

CLAM CHOWDER.—*Mrs. R. E. Cole.*

Fifty clams, two large slices of pork, one-third roll of butter, two dozen large potatoes, one-half pound of Boston crackers. Slice the potatoes thin; put them in a shallow pan with water enough to cover them; let them cook tender, but not enough to break by handling. Cut the black heads from the clams; cut the pork in small bits and fry brown; put a layer of clams onto the pork, then a layer of potatoes, then a layer of crackers (split open). Season with salt and pepper, and a portion of the butter; continue to do so until you have used all your material; pour over the whole the juice of the clams, and the water the potatoes were boiled in; then add enough hot milk to make a thin stew; it will take two or three quarts. Boil slowly five to eight minutes, watching carefully that it does not scorch. Longer cooking will make the clams tough.

RECIPE FOR CLAM CHOWDER—For a Family of Four.
Mrs. R. W. Snow.

Cut one-quarter pound salt pork in small pieces, put it into a kettle and brown, then add one sliced onion and let it brown; to this add four potatoes, cut in thin slices, season with pepper and salt cover this with water, and cook until soft; then add milk and the clam water, also three crackers; lastly, put in the clams and let the chowder come to a boil.

CRAB SOUP.—*Mrs. Dyer.*

One good-sized crab, to one quart of milk; take the white meat from the shell, and divide in small pieces; after boiling the milk, add the crab, and thicken with sifted crackers. When done add a spoonful of butter; season to taste with pepper and salt.

Use Kelsey & Flint's Flavoring Extracts.

DELMONICO'S RECIPE FOR OYSTER STEW.

Take one quart of liquid oysters; put the liquor (a teacupful for three) in a stew-pan, add half as much more water, salt, good bit of pepper, teaspoonful of rolled cracker for each. Put on the stove and boil; have your oysters ready in a bowl; the moment it begins to boil, pour in all your oysters—say ten for each person. Now watch carefully; as soon as it begins to boil, take out your watch, count just thirty seconds; take your oysters from the stove; have a large dish ready with one and one-half tablespoons of cold milk for each person; pour your stew on this milk, and serve immediately. Never boil an oyster in milk.

TOMATO SOUP.—*Mrs. A. L. Stone.*

One can of tomatoes, one quart of water, and one onion; strain and return to the kettle and add one pint of milk, two tablespoonfuls of browned flour, piece of butter the size of an egg, and salt and pepper. Strain into a tureen.

NICOLL, The Tailor.

JUST RECEIVED,

A fine assortment of Foreign and Domestic Woolens for this Season.

Call and see our New Patterns
- Suits to order, from...$20 00
- Pants to order, from....$5 00
- Overcoats to Order, from $20

Also, to accommodate our numerous country patrons visiting the city for a short time, I have added a splendid stock of

Men's, Boys' and Children's Ready-Made Suits and Overcoats,

Manufactured by ourselves, after the most approved and latest styles in custom-made patterns. Well cut, well made, stylish and cheap. You will do well to inspect before purchasing elsewhere. Civility to all. No trouble to show goods.

NICOLL, The Tailor,
Phelan's Building, 816-818 Market St., San Francisco

☞ BRANCH STORES IN ALL PRINCIPAL CITIES. ☜

FISH.

Fish can be scaled much easier by being laid in boiling water about a minute.

Salt fish are quickest and best freshened by soaking in sour milk.

Some varieties of fish that are very fine boiled or baked, are tasteless broiled or fried.

White fish are the best broiled, but very good boiled. Trout should always be boiled or baked; black bass, broiled if small; boiled when large; fresh mackerel should always be broiled; salmon, always be boiled; perch, smelt, brook trout and flounders are all better fried.

FISH A LA CRÉME.—*Mrs. Kellogg.*

Three pounds of fish, fresh cod, or any nice white fish; boil till tender, then remove the bones; mince it fine; season with salt, pepper and lemon. One quart of milk boiled with two onions until they are in shreds. Rub to a cream one-half pound of butter and two large tablespoonfuls of flour; turn the boiling milk through a sieve upon it, and return all to the saucepan; boil again, taking care to stir it so as to keep from burning or getting in lumps. Grate the rind of a lemon, and, with one-half a tumbler of wine, mix through the fish. Grate a loaf of bread through a colander; take the platter the fish is to be served on, and put first a layer of dressing on the dish, then the fish; repeat this until the dish is as full as you wish, making the top layer of dressing; then put the bread crumbs smoothly on the top, making an oval. Fill a bread-pan with water; put the platter upon it in the oven, and let it remain until it is a nice brown. When done put slices of parsley and lemon around it.

CUSK A LA CRÉME (Another way)—*Mrs. S. Richards.*

I use sturgeon, generally taking about two pounds. Rub the fish well with salt; put it into a kettle with enough boiling water to cover it. Put the juice of one lemon in the water. As soon as it boils, put it one side where it will just simmer. Let it stand for one hour; then take it up and draw out all the bones. Put one ounce of flour in a saucepan, to which add by degrees one quart of cream or milk, mixing it very smoothly; then add an onion, small, chopped very fine, a bunch of parsley, little nutmeg, salt and pepper. Put this on the fire, stirring till it forms a thick sauce. Stir in one-fourth pound of butter; strain sauce through the sieve; put some in bottom of the dish; lay fish in, and pour the rest of the sauce over it. Beat to a froth the whites of six eggs, and spread over the whole. Set in the oven and bake light brown.

FILLET OF SOLE AU GRATIN.—*Mrs. Chickering.*

Choose two flounders, weighing about three pounds. Lay them on the table with the dark side uppermost; with a sharp, thin-bladed knife cut down to the backbone, following the dark line in the middle of the fish, then turn the edge of the knife outward and cut towards the fins, keeping the blade flat against the bone, and removing one-fourth of the flesh of the fish in a single piece; proceed in the same way until you have eight fillets (this can be done at the fish market) carefully cut the skin from them, season with salt and pepper, lay them on a buttered dish, suitable to send to table, sprinkle thickly with sifted cracker crumbs, and a little grated Parmesan or any rich cheese; put a few bits of butter over them, using not more than one ounce, two tablespoonfuls in all, and brown them in a quick oven. Serve them as soon as they are nicely browned. This is a very savory and delicate dish, requiring some practice to do nicely, but comparatively inexpensive, and well worth all the trouble taken in making it.

CLUB-HOUSE FISH CAKES.—*Mrs. Chickering.*

Wash and boil one quart of potatoes, putting them on the fire in cold water enough to cover them, and a tablespoonful of salt. Put one and one-half pounds of salt codfish on the fire in plenty of cold water, and bring it slowly to a boil; as soon as it boils throw off that water, and put it again on the fire in fresh cold water; if the fish is very salt, change the water a third time. Free the fish from skin and bones; peel the potatoes, mash them through a colander with a potato masher, season with one-fourth saltspoonful of pepper, and one ounce of butter; add the yolks of two eggs, and the fish; mix well and make into cakes, using a little flour to prevent sticking to the hands. Fry them golden brown, in enough smoking hot fat to

Wm. K. Rowell, { Notary Public and Conveyancer, 458 Ninth St. Residence, 410 Thirteenth St., First House East of Broadway, Oakland.

nearly cover them; observe that in frying any article of food it will not soak fat if the latter be hot enough to carbonize the outside at once, and smoking hot fat will do that.

FRIED SOLE.—*Mrs. Wheeler.*

Remove the bones from a sturgeon; cut in slanting pieces about one-fourth of an inch thick, dip in beaten egg, roll in bread crumbs, cook by dropping into boiling lard. Use French mustard, oil and vinegar, beaten together for sauce.

FRIED FLOUNDER.

Dip the fish in milk, then in flour, then drop in boiling fat until brown.

SALT COD. (BY SPECIAL REQUEST.)

A favorite dish. Strip the fish, do not cut it. Freshen it by four or five hours' soaking. Place over the fire in a fish-kettle with plenty of cold water. The moment it boils remove to the back of the stove to simmer until tender. Never allow it to boil fast or the fish will eat hard and thready. Dish it upon a napkin, free from bones, and garnished with rings of hard boiled egg. Serve with egg sauce if you wish, but we prefer "pork scraps" fried a delicate brown. Potatoes, boiled onions, and beets are indispensable with this dish.

No more Flies, Dust or Rattling Windows!

T. BLACKBURN'S

Iron Corner, Ornamental

SLIDING FLY SCREENS

MADE TO ORDER.

Also, an Attachment for Windows and Doors to keep out Dust.

CALL OR ADDRESS,

531 EIGHTH STREET, - OAKLAND.

MEATS.

To choose good Beef see if it be of a bright red color in the lean part, and white in the fatty portions. Reject that which has yellowish suet, or spotted unequal surface.

Healthy Mutton is of a clear, darkish red. Lamb should have the kidney fresh and fat, and in the forequarter the vein should be blue. If you buy the shoulder have your butcher remove the bone to make a place for dressing.

Young Pork should be white and firm and dry. If it be darkish or soft to the touch, it is old and stale.

The desirable features of Veal are whiteness and fatness, which show that the calf was well fed and bled.

Choose your Chickens by seeing if the breast-bone yields to the touch, if the scales on the legs be smooth, and the comb red.

Select a Goose with a clean, white skin, plump breast, and yellow feet. If the feet are red the bird is old.

A young Turkey should have his legs black and smooth, his spurs short, and his feet limber.

Roasting.—Have a brisk oven, put only enough water in the pan to prevent burning; rub a very little flour over the joint, but neither salt nor pepper. Salt draws out the juices which it is your object to keep in, and parching injures the flavor of pepper. This applies also to broiling and frying. Always pepper after an article is cooked. Carefully turn your roast once that it may be browned on both sides.

The Gravy.—When the roast comes out put it on a hot dish, carefully pouring off the fat, then pour into the pan a little boiling water and salt, and with a spoon rub off all the dried gravy on the bottom and sides of the pan. Add no flour. The gravy should be thick enough with its own richness. If you have got your gravy too thin let it boil a few minutes.

Broiling.—A brisk, clear fire is indispensable to this mode of cooking. Let the gridiron come to a gradual heat that it may not be burning hot on the surface. Rub the bars with a bit of clean suet and lay on your steak or chop which should not be more than three-quarters of an inch in thickness. If too thick it will be overdone on

---

Dr. Merriman's { Fragrant Kalliodont, Beautifies, Preserves the Teeth, and Charms all who use it.

the outside while inside it is still raw. Turn it but once while broiling, and when it is a delicate brown outside with a rare line inside it is finished. Lay it on a well-heated platter and dress with butter and a little salt. If you have allowed your fire to get too low do not attempt to use the gridiron, but feed your fire anew, and if you cannot wait for it to burn low again, broil in a frying-pan following the same directions.

Boiling.—Never boil meat at a gallop. It injures the flavor and hardens the meat. Yet it must not go off the boil, as steeping gives meat an insipid taste.

Frying.—Professional cooks agree that the perfection of frying-fat is equal parts lard and beef drippings, and yet there are families where the drippings are never looked after, and all the rich fat from roast beef, pork, corn beef, and soup-bones goes to waste.

To Clarify It.—Put a little water in it, set it in boiling water and stir in a little salt. The next day it will turn out from a bowl in a solid cake. Scrape off the settlings and put it away for future use. It is as good as butter for shortening in cookies and ginger bread, and better than butter for meat frying.

Batter for Frying.—Three cups of sifted flour, mixed with three tablespoons of butter melted in warm water; pour the butter off the water into the flour first, then enough of the water to make a soft paste, which beat smooth, then more warm water till it is thick enough to mask the back of the spoon dipped into it, and salt to taste; add, the last thing, the whites of two eggs well beaten.

T. S. McCOOL. B. A. ARMSTRONG.

McCOOL & ARMSTRONG,

MANUFACTURERS AND IMPORTERS OF

PICTURE FRAME MOULDINGS,

ARTISTS' MATERIALS, PASSE-PARTOUTS, WINDOW CORNICES AND BRACKETS,

OIL PAINTINGS, STEEL ENGRAVINGS & CHROMOS.

Office and Factory, 411 Twelfth Street, Oakland, Cal.

BRANCH STORE, SAN FRANCISCO.

VEGETABLES.

All vegetables except potatoes, asparagus, peas, and cauliflower, should boil as fast as possible; these four only moderately. To prevent the bad odor arising from boiling cabbage, put it in plenty of boiling water, add a pinch of soda, cover closely, boil fast. Keep boiling for half an hour, no longer.

Onions should be boiled in milk and water. Equal parts.

Potatoes are the only vegeteable that should be put into cold water. They should be pared before being boiled, if you wish to have them mashed and look white. Pour off the water the minute they are done and stand on the back of the stove covered with a napkin. Sweet potatoes should not be pared, and they require longer cooking than the common potato.

Grate Gruyere's cheese on macaroni,
Make the top crisp, but not too bony.
Roast veal with rich stock gravy serve;
And pickled mushrooms, too, observe.
Roast pork, *sans* apple sauce, past doubt,
Is Hamlet with the Prince left out.
Your mutton chops with paper cover,
And make them amber brown all over.
Broil lightly your beefsteak—to fry it
Argues contempt of Christian diet.
Buy stall-fed pigeons; when you've got them
The way to cook them is to pot them.
It gives true epicures the vapors,
To see broiled mutton minus capers.
To roast spring chickens is to spoil 'em
Just split them down the back and broil 'em.
Boiled turkey, gourmands know, of course,
Is exquisite with Challenge Sauce.
Egg sauce—few make it right, alas!—
Is good with blue fish, or with bass.
Nice oyster sauce gives zest to cod;
A fish, when fresh, to feast a god.
Shad, stuffed and baked, is most delicious,
'Twould have electrified Apicius.

Swiss Confectionery, } **Ladies' and Gentlemen's Ice Cream and Coffee Saloon,**
416 Twelfth Street. Wm. J. F. Laage, Prop.

Breakfast and Lunch Dishes.

SCALLOPED POTATOES.—*Mrs. Sanford.*
A NICE BREAKFAST DISH.

Peel and slice raw potatoes very thin. Put them into a deep dish; a layer of potatoes with butter and salt, repeating until the dish is full. Pour in sweet milk till it may be seen at the edge of the dish by pressing down the potatoes. Bake half an hour in a quick oven.

POTATOES FOR LUNCH.

Take large, mealy potatoes, bake slowly until well done; carefully remove the inside by cutting an opening in one end, mash and season well with salt, pepper and cream; return to the skin and sew; place in the oven, and when very hot, send to the table.

STUFFED GREEN PEPPERS.—*Mrs. Dart.*

Cut the tops off the bell pepper, and remove the seed. Take two of the long green peppers, one small onion, one large tomato peeled, and chop all together very fine. Add stale bread crumbs sufficient to fill five peppers, a teaspoonful of salt, and sweet oil enough to moisten the whole. Fill the peppers and replace the tops. To be prepared on the day they are to be used.

SCALLOPED OYSTER PLANT.—*Mrs. Morse.*

Boil the oyster plant until perfectly tender, then take out of the water and rub through a colander. Add butter, pepper, salt and milk. Put in a baking dish and cover the top with bread crumbs, with here and there a small piece of butter. Set in the oven and bake a delicate brown.

DORMERS.—*Mrs. Van Blarcom.*

Two cups of cold mutton chopped fine, one cup boiled rice, a little suet, one egg, pepper and salt. Mix well the rice, meat, and

---

Get your Baking Powder of Kelsey & Flint.

suet, with high seasoning of pepper and salt. Make into balls; dip them into the beaten egg, and cover with bread crumbs. Fry in hot drippings a nice brown. Serve with a little made gravy poured over them.

CORN OYSTERS.—*Mrs. Carpenter.*

Twelve ears of sweet corn grated, one teaspoon salt, one teaspoon pepper, two eggs beaten into two spoons flour. Mix well and fry brown butter or sweet lard

BAKED CAULIFLOWER.—*Mrs. Wheeler.*

Boil until tender in salt and water, then drain and place in a dripping-pan with butter or nice drippings in the bottom; season with pepper and salt, add bread crumbs and cheese sprinkled over the cauliflower; then baste with melted butter, and bake slowly in the oven till a nice brown.

TOMATO MACARONI.—*Mrs. R. E. Cole..*

ITALIAN STYLE.

Cook a quart of tomatoes until quite dry; season with salt, pepper and butter. Cook your macaroni till tender, and drain it. Small cup of cheese grated or chopped fine (Swiss cheese is best.) Melt a piece of butter in a spider and stir in the cheese till ropy. Turn the tomatoes into it and season with red pepper. Pour this over the macaroni, serve hot. Splendid for lunch.

BAKED TOMATOES.—*Mrs. Brewer.*

Butter a dish and lay the skimmed tomatoes in whole. Sprinkle salt, pepper and sugar over them, and then cover with fine bread or cracker crumbs. Bake forty minutes in a dish in which they may go upon the table. When half done dip the syrup over the top to moist the crumbs.

SCRAPPLE.—*Mrs. E. P. Flint.*

Take ten pounds of pork (fat and lean), boil it well, take out all the bones, and chop it rather fine; return the meat to the water in which it was boiled, and add equal parts corn meal and buckwheat flour until very thick. Season well with salt, pepper and sage; boil twenty minutes, put in pans to cool; cut in thin slices, and fry a dark brown.

VEAL AND HAM PRESSED.—*Mrs. J. T. Agard.*
TO EAT COLD.

Equal quantities of veal and ham slices one-fourth inch thick. Butter a dish, lay in a slice of veal, season with salt and pepper; then a slice of ham with pepper; continue to alternate till all is used. Cover with a crust of flour and water. Steam three hours. Slice when cold.

TONGUE WITH JELLY.—*Mrs Palache.*

Use either a fresh corned or a smoked tongue. If fresh, add a small teacup of salt; boil until very tender; trim and place in a bowl that will just hold it, and a teacup of jelly made by the following recipe: Put a fine, plump chicken in a saucepan with a pot of cold water. When very tender, remove choicest parts for a salad, and return remnants to the pan for a second boiling. When reduced to one teacup, strain, season to taste, and pour over tongue. Put to press with good weight in a cool place.

BONED CHICKEN.—*Mrs. E. S. Cole.*

Boil a chicken in a little soup stock until the bones can be easily separated from the meat; remove all the skin; slice and mix the light and dark meat; season with salt and pepper; boil down the juice and pour it on the meat, and shape it like a loaf of bread. Wrap tightly in a cloth; press with a heavy weight for a few hours. When served, cut in thin slices.

STEWED CRAB.—*Mrs. Israel Knox.*

Take the meat from one boiled crab, rub one teaspoonful flour in one large tablespoonful butter, add one-half cup of cream or milk. Season high with red pepper and salt; boil to thicken, not over five minutes.

Buy your Fish of Edwards Bros. 468 Eleventh St.

HOT CRAB.—*Mrs. E. S. Cole.*

Carefully pick out the inside of a crab and the large claws, and mince them, mixing these thoroughly and seasoning with cayenne pepper and salt. Rub up a small teaspoonful of good curry powder in a little cold gravy or cream, or equal proportions of both, and mix these with the crab, adding a teaspoonful of Chile vinegar, and some finely-grated bread crumbs. Clean out the shell very carefully and put the mixture in it, sifting bread crumbs over it, and a little butter. Brown well.

DEVILED CRAB.—*Mrs. S. Woods.*

Remove meat from crab and pick very fine. Make a cream sauce of a pint of milk or cream, one large tablespoonful of flour, add a speck of cayenne pepper, and a little salt; one-half cup of bread crums, two hard-boiled eggs, chopped fine. Mix all together with cream sauce, add juice of one lemon. After it is in the shell, sprinkle with crumbs, and put little bits of butter on.

BAKED OMELETTE.—*Mrs. Coxhead.*

Three gills of milk, piece of butter size of walnut; bring to a scald; five eggs, yolks and whites beaten separately, a little salt, a teaspoonful of flour wet to a smooth paste in milk. Pour milk in, stirring constantly; then stir in the paste, put in buttered dish, bake in a moderate oven twenty minutes,

BAKED OMELETTE.—*Mrs. J. K. McLean.*

One-half cup of milk put on to boil. Stir in the well-beaten yolks of six eggs till thick. A dessertspoonful of butter. Salt to taste. After removing from the fire add whites of six eggs, well beaten. The oven should be heated as for cake. Bake ten minutes.

BREAD OMELETTE.—*Mrs. Everett.*

Yolks of six eggs, cup of milk, season with salt and pepper, stir in the whites beaten stiff. Now stir in a cup of powdered cracker. Cook in a frying-pan or on a griddle with as little butter as possible, then lay a hot dish over it and turn over the omelette on the dish.

If you want { Good Stamping for Embroidery, go to Miss J. S. Naismith's; 1161 Broadway.

The advantage of bread omelette is that it will keep tender till cold while others grow tough if not eaten at once.

NICE BREAKFAST DISH.—*Mrs. E. S. Cole.*

Bits of nice salt pork about one-third of an inch thick, two or three inches square, bits of calf's liver the same size. Put these alternately on a long skewer, beginning and ending with pork. Lay it in the oven across a dripping-pan and roast as you would a bird, basting occasionally. When done, slide the pieces from a skewer and serve on a hot plate.

BAKED MEAT STEW.—*Mrs. Niswander.*

Cut any sort of cold meat, but roast beef is best, into thin slices, cover the bottom of an earthen baking-dish, and season with salt, pepper, sage or summer savory, and a very little chopped red pepper or cayenne; cover with a layer of chopped onion, then another layer of meat, and so on until the dish is half filled, then pour in tomatoes, either fresh or canned, to fill the dish; if the meat be very lean put in bits of butter with the seasoning, but cold gravy is better poured on the tomatoes. Cover with a tight-fitting plate, and cook in the oven slowly for two hours. To make an ornamental dish, put potatoes very smoothly mashed and seasoned around a meat dish, like a wall about three inches high; brush with the yellow of an egg and set in the oven to brown a little, then pour the stew inside.

VEAL LOAF.—*Mrs. Niswander.*

Three and one-half pounds of veal, not too young, chopped finely, five small crackers rolled, one tablespoon salt, one teaspoon pepper, one-half nutmeg, three beaten eggs; mix thoroughly together with the hand, using only one-fourth of the rolled crackers, forming into an oval loaf and pressing it together as firmly as possible. Spot it thickly with bits of butter, and strew over the rest of the crackers. Lay in a dripping-pan with a little water and let it cook slowly for two hours, basting occasionally and adding water from time to time so that there may be a gravy when done. It should be well done; but if the browning is too rapid, turn over it a greased pan. Nice when cold.

The Travelers { Is paying at the rate of over $2,000 per day for Injuries.

CLAM PIE.—*Mrs. Edwards.*

One quart clams chopped fine ; place in a deep dish withont bottom crust. Season with pepper and butter. Thicken with flour or cracker dust, place on top three thin slices of salt pork ; then cover over with ordinary pie crust ; bake thirty minutes.

CLAM FRITTERS.—*Mrs. Edwards.*

One quart clams, chop very fine, one teacup flour, one teaspoonful yeast powder, mixed well with the clams ; season to suit taste ; fry in hot fat.

BOILED BEEF—(Pressed.)—*Mrs. Niswander.*

Ten pounds good beef, rib piece preferred ; put in a saucepan with two quarts cold water and a small half cup salt. Cook slowly till very tender, taking care that the water does not entirely evaporate, then remove bone, gristle and skinny parts, cut the lean and fat to mix equally and season highly with pepper and more salt if necessary; put in a bowl with a heavy weight in a cool place.

OYSTER CAKES.—*Mrs. Brewer.*

FOR BREAKFAST.

One can oysters, four medium-sized potatoes, butter the size of an egg, two soda, or six small crackers, salt, pepper. Take the oysters from the liquor and chop fine ; boil and mash the potatoes, moisten with part of the liquor, and butter, salt and pepper, and part of crackers ; mix all together and make into little cakes ; roll each one in cracker crumbs, and fry in plenty of hot fat.

OYSTER FRICASSEE.—*Mrs. A. L. Stone.*

One quart of oysters, drain off the juice and strain it ; make a pint of the liquid by adding water or milk ; add one tablespoonful of butter, one of flour, little pepper, salt and mace, boil all together, then put in the oysrers and cook very little ; have ready three eggs, well beaten, one tablespoon lemon juice and one tablespoon chopped parsley, and turn on to the oysters when removed from the fire; serve on slices of toast.

Dr Merriman's { Fragrant Kalliodont Beautifies and Preserves the Teeth.

CREAMED OYSTERS.—*Mrs. S. Woods.*

One generous tablespoon of flour, one pint cream, one piece of onion size of a dime, one very small piece of mace, one pint of oysters, salt, and pepper to taste. Let the cream come to a boil with onion and mace; mix flour with a little cold milk, stir into the boiling cream, cook eight minutes. Let the oysters come to a boil in their own liquor, drain and add them to the cream, having first skimmed out the onion and mace. Season to taste and serve on toast.

SCALLOPED OYSTERS.—*Mrs. McLean.*

Butter a baking-dish, put a layer of cracker crumbs or rolled cracker in the bottom, then a layer of oysters well seasoned with pepper and salt, with pieces of butter, another layer of crumbs and so on till the dish is filled, putting on each layer of crumbs, oyster, liquor and milk. The top layer should be of crumbs with abundance of butter and milk. Some prefer bread crumbs as they are more moist.

FRIED OYSTERS.—*Mrs. A. M. Green.*

Drain large oysters through a sieve; beat two eggs; have ready grated bread crumbs; sprinkle salt and a little pepper over the oysters; dip each one in the egg and cover with bread crumbs; put equal portions of lard and butter in a hot frying-pan, when boiling hot lay in oysters carefully; give close attention to prevent burning or too much cooking. Serve hot.

FRIED CHICKEN.—*Mrs. N. G. Dow.*

WITH CREAM GRAVY.

Leave the breast whole, also the back, wings and legs, making in all six pieces. For three chickens have ready one gill sifted flour; add one-half teaspoon each of salt and pepper. Roll each piece in flour, fry in hot lard and butter, equal proportions of each, one-third of an inch deep. As they brown, turn; when cooked, arrange breasts side by side, the backs beneath, surround with legs and wings. Make a gravy of one pint sweet cream, one and one-half tablespoons flour, rub smooth in cream, one-half teaspoon salt, peper and parsley. Put in the lard and let simmer; pour hot over the chicken.

Pure Cream Tartar at Kelsey & Flint's.

FRICASSEE CHICKEN.—*Mrs. N. G. Dow.*

Cut the neck from the body, then the wings, then cut in two lengthwise through the sides; stew, but not serve the neck. The liver is good. Place in a kettle with one-half pint water, tablespoonful of vinegar, an onion grated, pepper and salt; cover closely; stew three-quarters of an hour; add one and one-half ounce butter, one spoonful chopped parsley, and just before taking up, add a beaten egg.

DUMPLINGS FOR POTPIE.—*Mrs. Craig.*

One cup sweet milk, two teaspoons yeast powder, a little salt, flour enough to make a batter that will drop from a spoon, one egg, beating the white to a froth and stir in last; then butter a pie tin and drop the batter on with the spoon; put in a steamer and cover close; steam thirty minutes. Do not check the boiling for an instant, nor remove the cover; follow the directions and they will come out like snowballs.

HAM SANDWICHES.—*Mrs. Pitman.*

QUICKLY MADE.

Four baker's loaves, two cans deviled ham, one roll butter (for spreading). This makes 125 sandwiches. Cut off end of loaf (heel not used), spread the open end with butter, scant, then spread on ham; slice; next spread open end of loaf with butter without the ham; slice, and place the two buttered sides together; cut across the middle, making two sandwiches. Spread loaf again, and proceed as before. By this process the bread can be spread very thin. If preferred, use finely-chopped lean ham dressed with mustard; butter and cream can be used and the crust of the bread cut carefully away.

HAM SANDWICHES, No. 2.

Take the yolks of two hard-boiled eggs, three tablespoonfuls of prepared mustard, and stir them with one-half pound butter, to a cream. Spread your bread, which must be cut thin, with this dressing, and put on it finely-chopped ham, entirely free from fat.

CURRIED VEAL.—*Mrs. Everett.*

Have ready two pounds veal cutlet, cut in pieces; several slices salt pork, one large onion sliced thin. Stew the cutlets gently, in water enough to cover them, until tender. Set aside; keep warm. Fry out the slices of pork and in the fat fry the onion very brown and remove (not served). Now brown the stewed cutlets in this fat and place them in the center of a large platter; keep hot. Next, stir the liquor from the stew and the pork fat together; let it boil up and then thicken with three teaspoons curry powder; add a little lemon juice or a little vinegar, and pour the gravy thus made over the platter, having previously piled around the meat a border of boiled rice (the only vegetable needed with this dish).

To boil the Rice.—Twenty minutes before serving wash thoroughly two cups of rice, and throw into two quarts of boiling water; add a little salt, and boil until tender; the grains should be whole and separate, and quite white, which is always the case when plenty of water is used. Chicken can be curried in the same manner, using butter if preferred, instead of pork.

BEEF A LA DAUBE.—*Mrs. Israel Knox.*

For a family of six, take three pounds of a round of beef, season highly with salt, black pepper and cayenne, fry a few slices of pork in the bottom of your kettle until a very light brown; dredge the seasoned meat thickly with flour, place in the kettle with a piece of butter the size of a walnut, and a few slices of onion and carrot; add no liquid. Cover very close so the steam cannot escape, and steam slowly three or four hours. Serve with rice.

A LA MODE BEEF.—*Miss Perkins.*

Chop an onion, half a carrot, half a turnip, a little parsley and celery, and place in a round-bottom kettle, together with one-quarter of a pound of fat salt pork, one tablespoonful butter, a little pepper, salt and sage. Upon these place three pounds of beef, cut from the upper part of the round, well dredged with flour, and fry until brown; turn the meat often. Add about a quart of boiling water, cover, and simmer gently about three hours. Strain the gravy over the meat, having first skimmed off all the fat, and serve. The dish may be garnished with potato balls or butter onions.

CHICKEN PIE.—*Mrs. Wheeler.*

Take two good-sized chickens and prepare as for stewing. Cover

---

J. Letter, Gentlemen's Furnishing Goods, 1001 Broadway.

with water, season with salt and pepper, and boil gently until the bones slip from the meat. Take out the chicken and thicken the liquor with a little flour. Remove the large bones from the fowl; have ready a paste made as for strawberry short-cake; line a six-quart milk-pan with the paste, and partially bake before filling. Then add the chicken and gravy; put on the upper crust slit several times, wet over the top with milk, and bake slowly until it is a nice brown.

CHICKEN PIE.—*Mrs. J. C. Hays.*

Two nice tender chickens, one sweet-bread, two dozen raw oysters, one onion, half a dozen small peppers (size of a pea). Stew the chickens with the peppers and onion. (The latter must be taken out whole). Season with salt, pepper and butter. Thicken with flour and set aside to cool. Stew the sweet-bread, and when cold, cut in slices. Make a nice puff paste, line your dish and place a cup in the center; next lay the chicken and sweet-bread in the dish, and stew the oysters evenly over them; cover with upper crust; make small holes near the center, and bake.

BAKED BEANS.

Soak one quart of small pea beans over night, next morning parboil them, pour off the water, add more, and cook until they are a little tender; place in a deep dish, season with salt and one tablespoonful of molasses. Take one pound of pork, partly lean, score and conceal, except the rind, in the middle of the beans, cover with boiling water and bake from four to six hours. If the beans become dry add more water.

DIAMONDS.   **FRENCH CLOCKS.**

S. LATHROP,
Practical Watchmaker and Jeweler,

DEALER IN
Watches, Clocks, Jewelry
AND
SILVERWARE,

1059 Broadway,
Between Eleventh and
Twelfth Streets,
OAKLAND, CAL.

WHITE BREAD!
NICE BREAD!

Horace Davis & Co's

BEST ROLLER MILL FLOUR.

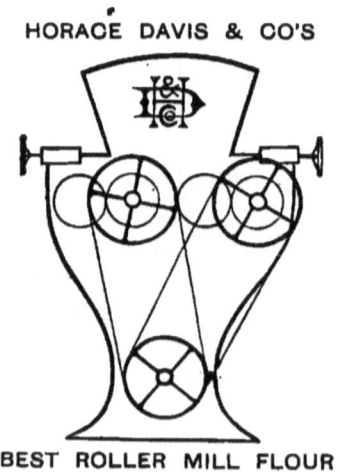

(THIS CUT IS ON EVERY BAG.)

BREAD.

RULES FOR BREAD MAKING.

Do not mix the dough too stiff. *Remember* it should be as soft as can be handled.

Keep it warm enough while rising. *Remember* a chill is fatal to your sponge.

Allow it long enough time to rise. *Remember* the old couplet,

"Half-raised bread,
Putty and lead."

Twice its bulk is a good rule for a second rising.

FAMILY BREAD.—*Mrs. Israel Knox.*

I use, and can conscientiously recommend, Horace Davis and Co's Best Roller Mill Flour. It is what it professes to be—the cream of wheat. To one quart of sweet milk, take one-third of a compressed yeast cake, and three teaspoonfuls of white sugar; stir in flour until you have a dough so stiff that it will not run or drop from a spoon; set it in a moderately warm room and let it rise until morning; then put flour on your kneading-board, mold your loaves about two inches thick; and put in pans (handling as little as possible) and let it rise again. When ready for the oven prick the loaves through to the bottom with a fork; bake half an hour. When taken from the oven, roll lightly in a bread-cloth until cool. I use a piece of flannel or old tablecloth.

In the morning if you wish delicious gems, dip with a spoon some of this same dough and fill your gem pans two-thirds full and bake for breakfast. Ten or fifteen minutes will bake them a beautiful brown. Thus from this same dough you have both bread and gems that are delicious, without shortening of any kind. If you wish hot biscuits for lunch, you have only to save a small portion of this dough, roll it thin, and spread with butter or shortening, fold it a few times, using all the time just flour enough to handle, roll to about half an inch thick, and put in your pans and let rise again, which takes two or three hours. Your biscuit will bake in from seven to ten minutes, and unless you wish the crust very crisp, fold in a napkin and send to the table.

A Toilet { Is incomplete without Dr. Merriman's Fragrant Kalliodont.

POTATO YEAST.

Six Irish potatoes, peeled and grated, one cup sugar, one-half cup salt; pour over these about one quart of boiling water, enough to cover them; when cool, add one pint yeast, and set away to rise. This recipe will make about six bottles of yeast.

PARKER HOUSE ROLLS.—*Mrs. Niswander.*

Scald one pint of milk, stir in one heaping tablespoonful of shortening, one teaspoonful of salt; when lukewarm pour into one quart of sifted flour, mixed with one teacupful of white sugar; dissolve one-third of a cake of compressed yeast in a little milk and stir in with flour sufficient to make a stiff batter; when light knead for fifteen minutes; when raised again, knead for five minutes; make into small rolls and when very light, bake.

LIGHT ROLLS.—*Mrs. S. Woods.*

Scald one quart of milk, melt in it a piece of butter the size of an egg; when cool add one egg well beaten, one-half or two-thirds cake of German Compressed Yeast dissolved in milk (the sponge will rise quicker if two-thirds of the cake is used); a little salt, tablespoonful sugar. Thicken with flour to a batter as thick as muffin batter. Let it rise, and when light add flour to mold lightly. Let it rise again, then roll out and spread melted butter over the top; cut out and fold together; let it rise the third time, and bake in a quick oven ten minutes. The oven must be hot; much depends on baking.

If one-half the milk is used, and when scalded, cold water is added to make the quart, the rolls will be lighter and more delicate for the first day, but are dry and stale the next day.

BEATEN BISCUIT.—*Mrs. Clarke.*

One pint flour, tablespoon lard, a little salt; water sufficient to make a soft dough; work it long and well with the hands or beat it with the rolling-pin, on this depends the lightness and excellence; roll about an inch thick, cut with biscuit cutter; bake in a quick oven.

Cure for Consumption, at Fish & Co's, Eighth and Market.

NEW MILK BREAD.—*Mrs. Parsons.*

One pint new milk, one pint boiling water poured on the milk, flour as thick as for fritters, set in a warm place (not hot enough to harden the dough on the bottom of the pan). After it has foamed up add a little salt, and knead with as little flour as possible. Put in pans and let it rise again about twenty minutes, and bake.

BISCUIT FOR A SMALL FAMILY.—*Mrs. Craig.*

One cup sweet milk, half a teaspoonful salt, three tablespoons melted butter or sweet lard, two and a half cups flour, three teaspoons baking powder. Bake immediately. (Makes one dozen). Drop biscuit can be made the same way by adding less flour and dropping from a spoon on a buttered tin. .

SODA BISCUIT.—*Mrs. Nugent.*

Sift into one quart of flour, two heaping teaspoons baking powder; stir it through, then rub in a piece of butter the size of an egg, and one-half teaspoon of salt; mix lightly with water or sweet milk, as soft as it can be rolled out; roll quite quick, and cut with a small cutter· Bake in a quick oven.

SALLY LUNN.—*Mrs. Carpenter.*

Beat two eggs very light, over which pour one cup of sweet milk, one-third cup of sugar, two tablespoons melted butter, a little salt two cups of flour, and three teaspoons baking powder. Bake in a moderate oven.

MUSH MUFFINS.—*Mrs. Flint.*

Take one quart warm Indian meal mush, piece of butter as large as an egg; thin it with milk, about one pint, then thicken it with wheat flour, a little salt; make it as thick as you can well stir it, put in your yeast, and set to rise. Bake in muffin rings.

MUFFINS.—*Mrs. Woods.*

Four cups flour, two cups of milk quite warm, two eggs, butter size of a walnut, one good tablespoonful of yeast, one teaspoonful of

---

Buy your Fish of Edwards Bros. 468 Eleventh St.

sugar with the eggs. Let it rise a few minutes in the tins or bake immediately in muffin rings.

WAFFLES.

The same as for muffins, only a little less flour, and more butter, the cups not quit so full.

POPOVERS.—*Mrs. Agard.*

One cup milk, one cup flour, salt; mix together and add two eggs well beaten. Bake in gem irons. To be eaten with sauce.

SQUASH GRIDDLE CAKES.—*Mrs. R. E. Cole.*

One cup squash boiled and strained through a colander, two eggs, one quart of milk, a pinch of salt, flour to make it of a consistency for frying, one-half teaspoon yeast powder; wet up over night, and in the morning stir in one-eighth teaspoon of soda dissolved in water.

BUCKWHEAT CAKES.—*Mrs. E. P. Flint.*

Take lukewarm water and add buckwheat sufficient to make a very thick batter; put in your yeast with a little salt, beat a long time. Just before frying them add one-half teacup milk with one-half teaspoonful soda dissolved in it. Put in as gently as possible without stirring the batter.

CORN CAKES.—*Mrs. E. S. Cole.*

FOR BREAKFAST.

One egg, one-half cup sugar, one cup sour cream, one of corn meal, one of flour, one-half teaspoon soda.

CORN BREAD.—*Mrs. Luke Doe.*

Two cups of flour, one cup of corn meal, two eggs, two large spoons of sugar, one large spoon of melted butter, two spoons of yeast powder, salt, and milk enough to make a thin batter; bake in gem pans.

BROWN BREAD.—*Mrs. R. E. Cole.*

One pint bowl of corn meal, one pint bowl of rye meal, small coffeecup full of molasses, heaping teaspoonful of soda, salt. Pour your molasses over your meal, add salt, and then wet it quite soft with sour milk; dissolve the soda in boiling water and stir it the last thing. Put it in a vessel with a tight cover, and steam four or five hours. A large loaf will require *six* or more hours.

BAKED BROWN BREAD.—*Mrs. Sackrider.*

Three cups corn meal, two cups rye meal, three-quarters of a cup of molasses, one egg, one quart sweet milk, one tablespoonful of lard, a little salt, two heaping teaspoonfuls of yeast powder; bake in a tin pudding dish or a lard pail, closely covered; for three hours slowly.

BOSTON BROWN BREAD.—*Mrs. S. T. Fisher.*

One egg, one-third cup sugar, one pint sour milk, one and one-half cups white flour, two cups corn meal, two teaspoonfuls soda, a little salt. When prepared put it in a buttered pan *immediately* over *boiling* water. Steam three hours or more; bake one-half an hour. This will be good without the egg.

BROWN BREAD.—*Mrs. Kellogg.*

Three and one-half small cups milk, one cup molasses, three cups corn meal, one cup Graham, one cup white flour, one teaspoonful soda, salt. Steam four hours, then bake fifteen minutes.

GRAHAM BREAD.—*Mrs. Coxhead.*

Two quarts Graham flour, one pint fine flour, one cup molasses, teaspoonful of salt, and one-fourth of a cake compressed yeast. Stir together at night with little more than a quart of lukewarm water, or milk and water; in the morning when light, knead and mold into loaves the same as white bread, only *very soft*. When light (but not too light) bake a little longer time than white bread.

CORN BREAD.—*Miss Perkins.*

Two cnps of corn meal, one cup of Graham or white flour, one-half cup of molasses, one egg, one cup of sour milk in which is dissolved one teaspoonful of soda. Mix very thin with sweet milk. Put a little melted butter in the pan. Bake about ten minutes in a hot oven.

(For other bread and breakfast cakes, see "Chapter for Dyspeptics.")

Miss E. S. Buell, { Decorative Art Rooms. Fancy Work of all Kinds. 1118 Washington Street, Oakland.

Melrose Baking Powder.

ALWAYS PURE! FULL WEIGHT AND FULL STRENGTH!

Housekeepers who want good, healthy Bread, delicious Biscuits, Cakes or Muffins should use

MELROSE BAKING POWDER.

It contains none of the poisonous ingredients so commonly used in baking powders to increase the weight.

MELROSE is a pure Cream Tartar and Soda Baking Powder, it contains

NO STARCH, AMMONIA OR ALUM!

ONE TRIAL will convince any housekeeper of its superiority over all other baking powders.

Wellman, Peck & Co.,

126 to 132 Market St., and 23 and 25 California St., San Francisco.

CAKE.

RULES EOR CAKE.

Have the ingredients all measured and prepared and the tins prepared and buttered before mixing materials.

Sift the cream of tartar, or baking powder, well into the flour; be sure that the baking powder is pure. We heartily recommend the "Melrose." Dissolve the soda in the milk, or, if no milk is used, in a little warm water.

Roll the sugar; beat the butter to a cream; mix butter and sugar together.

Beat the yolks and whites of the eggs separately, and add them gradually to the butter and sugar.

Next add the milk, if used, or the dissolved soda, not using the dregs Last the prepared flour, stir as little as possible after adding the flour.

When fruit is used it should be dredged with flour, and added the last thing.

Cake to be light should be baked slowly at first, until the batter is evenly heated all through.

Cake is much more delicate made with pulverized sugar than with a coarser kind.

Eggs will beat lighter and quicker if they are put in a basin of cold water half an hour before using.

REPUBLICAN CAKE.—*Mrs. E. S. Cole.*

One pound flour, one pound sugar, one-half pound butter, four eggs, one teacup sour cream, one-half teaspoon soda, coffeecup raisins, one-half a nutmeg, a little mace.

IMPERIAL CAKE.—*Mrs. E. S. Cole.*

One pound of butter, one pound powdered sugar, one pound flour, one pound raisins, one pound sweet almonds blanched and cut thin, one-half pound citron cut thin, ten eggs, one nutmeg. Beat the butter and sugar and cream, then the eggs thoroughly and add next, then

---

Get all your Fancy Work done at Miss Naismith's, 1161 Broadway.

the sifted flour; sprinkle the fruit lightly with flour before adding to the mixture. It requires to be well baked. Half the recipe makes a good-sized loaf.

MYRTLE CAKE.—*Mrs. Richards.*

Five eggs, beaten lightly, three cups sugar, one cup butter beaten with the sugar, one cup milk, four cups sifted flour, grated rind of one lemon, small teaspoon soda. This will make two good-sized loaves.

POUND CAKE.—*Mrs E. S. Cole.*

One pound flour, one pound sugar, three-fourths pound butter, nine eggs, three of the whites out, one spoonful rose water.

LITTLE POUND CAKES.—*Miss Flint.*

A good three-fourths cup butter, one cup white sugar, two cups flour, three eggs beaten separately, one teaspoon baking powder, one half cup milk, little nutmeg, and one teaspoon bitter almonds.

NEW ENGLAND ELECTION CAKE.—*Mrs. E. S. Cole.*

Two cups good strong yeast, three cups milk, two cups sugar. Flour to make a very stiff batter with the hand. Let it rise over night. In the morning add three cups of sugar and two of butter (some prefer one of butter and one of lard), mix to a cream, two nutmegs, one teaspoon pulverized mace. Let it rise. When well risen pour it into the baking pans, adding a large bowl of stoned raisins and citron. Rise well and bake one hour.

CORN STARCH CAKE.—*Mrs. Porter.*

Whites of three eggs well beaten, one cup of sugar, one-half cup of butter, one cup of milk, half cup corn starch, two cups of flour, one teaspoonful of cream tartar and half teaspoonful of soda, flavor with lemon.

SPRINGFIELD CREAM PUFFS.—*Mrs. A. P. Flint.*

Two cups of water, one cup of butter, two cups of flour. Boil the butter and water together, and stir in the flour while boiling.

E. A. Brown, { **Wholesale and Retail Dealer in Wood and Coal, 410 and 412 Ninth Street.**

When cool add six eggs, not beaten, and stir well. Drop in pans the size of an egg. Have a quick oven; bake twenty-five minutes; avoid opening the oven while baking. Cream for the above—two cups of milk, one cup of sugar, three-fourths cup of flour, two eggs beaten with the sugar. Add the flour, and stir into the milk while boiling. Flavor with vanilla.

SNOW DROPS.—*Mrs. Everett.*

One cup butter, two cups sugar, whites of five eggs, one-half cup milk, three cups flour, two teaspoons yeast powder. Bake in small round tins and frost. (Pretty for children's parties).

MOUNTAIN CAKE.—*Mrs. Agard.*

One cup sugar, one-half cup butter, one-half cup milk, two cups flour, two eggs, one teaspoon cream tartar, one-half teaspoon soda, nutmeg. Suggestion—Frosting will keep a long time without hardening, if two or three spoonfuls of dissolved gelatine is stirred in when making.

HARRISON CAKE.—*Mrs. Brewer.*

To two cups molasses, add one of brown sugar, one of butter, one of sour cream or milk, one of raisins seeded, one of currants, and half a cup citron; a teaspoon each of clove, cinnamon, allspice and nutmeg, and two (small) saleratus. To mix it, cut the butter in little pieces, and put into a saucepan with the molasses; when the molasses boils up, pour it immediately upon 3½ cups of flour, and add the sugar and half the cream; stir it well; then add the saleratus, the rest of the cream, the spice, and flour enough to make it the consistency of cup cake, and last the fruit. Bake rather slowly. All cake containing molasses is more liable to burn than that which has none.

FRUIT CAKE.—*Mrs. Everett.*

One pound of butter beaten to a cream, one pound fine sugar added by degrees and well beaten. Ten well-beaten eggs added gradually. Beat till light; then add one pound sifted flour, three pounds well-dried currants, three pounds stoned raisins, two ounces citron, grated rind of a lemon, extract of almond or lemon if preferred, one ounce cloves, two ounces cinnamon, one nutmeg.

Oakland Transfer Co. } **San Francisco Office,** 3 Post St. 28 Market St.

SUNSHINE CAKE.—*Mrs. Chickering.*

Yolks of eleven eggs, one cup of butter, one cup of milk; two cups of sugar, three cups of flour, one teaspoon of cream tartar, half teaspoon of soda.

VANILLA CAKE.—*Mrs. Brewer.*

One-half cup butter, one and one-half cups sugar, one and one-half cups flour, one-half cup corn starch, one-half cup sweet milk, three eggs, two teaspoons yeast powder, one teaspoon vanilla; stir the corn starch with the butter and sugar, and then add the milk, flour, etc., the whites of eggs beaten to a froth last. This makes nice gold and silver cake, by using the whites and yolks separately of six eggs. The other proportions remain the same.

POOR MAN'S CAKE.—*Mrs. M. S. Root.*

Two and one-half cups of flour, three eggs, two cups of sugar, one cup of milk, four tablespoons of melted butter, one teaspoon of soda, two of cream tartar.

RIBBON CAKE.—*Mrs. Niswander.*

Five eggs, reserving two whites for icing, one and one-half common-sized teacup sugar, three-fourths cup butter, not pressed down tightly, one-half cup cold water, three teaspoons baking powder sifted into two cups flour, slightly heaped. Divide the batter, which should be thin, as nearly equal as possible, add to one-half the mixture a teaspoon each of allspice and cinnamon, one-half nutmeg, and one cup currants. Bake in four layers, two of each color, and lay alternately, with icing between.

MARBLE CAKE.—*Mrs. Richardson.*

White part—The whites of four eggs, one cup of powdered white sugar, one-half cup butter, one-half cup sweet milk, one-half teaspoonful soda, one teaspoonful cream tartar, one and one-half cups flour.

Black part—The yolks of the four eggs, one cup brown sugar, one-half cup molasses, one-half cup sour milk, one-half cup butter, one teaspoonful soda, one and one-half cups flour. Spices to suit the taste. Put first into the pan a layer of white and then a layer of black. Much improved by a thick layer of icing.

COFFEE CAKE.—California Recipe Book.

One and a half cups of molasses, one cup of brown sugar, one cup of butter, one and a half cups of strong coffee; one teaspoon of soda, two eggs, one cup of raisins and one of currants; spice as you like; flour to make as stiff as cup cake. Nice.

DRIED APPLE CAKE.—*Mrs. Brett.*

Three cups of dried apples soaked over night. Chop fine and cook with two cups of sugar one-half an hour, then cool; then add this to one cup of butter, one cup of brown sugar, three eggs, four cups of flour, all kinds of spice, salt two level teaspoons of soda, two level teaspoons cream of tartar, one cup of raisins and one quarter pound of citron.

RAISED OR BREAD CAKE.—*Mrs. Agard.*

Two cups light dough, one cup butter, two cups sugar, three eggs, one large cup raisins, one-half teaspoon soda, one teaspoon cinnamon, nutmeg. Beat the eggs very light, and add after working in the butter, sugar, soda and spices. Stir in the fruit and more flour if necessary. Bake at once.

SPONGE CAKE.—*Mrs. E. S. Cole.*

One pound sugar, nine eggs beaten three-fourths of an hour, three-fourths pound flour, one glass rosewater, juice and peel of one lemon; peel first.

SPONGE CAKE.—*Mrs. Knowles.*

Four eggs, one cup sugar, four tablespoonfuls water, one cup flour, one teaspoonful lemon, one teaspoonful yeast powder. Beat yolks and sugar to a cream, add water, then flour and yeast powder, beat; add whites already beaten to stiff froth, lemon. Bake twenty minutes.

The Travelers { Has issued 846,452 Accident Policies, and paid 84,761 Claims.

WHITE SPONGE CAKE.—*Mrs. Buck.*

One and one-half tumbler sugar (pulverized), one tumbler flour, one-half teaspoonful salt, one teaspoonful cream tartar, whites of ten eggs, beaten to a stiff froth. Sift sugar, flour, salt and cream tartar five times through a flour sieve. Add gradually to the eggs, beating lightly, flavor to taste. Bake in a very slow oven forty minutes; first twenty must not brown.

BERWICK.—*Mrs. Brewer.*

Beat six eggs, yolks and whites together two minutes; add three cups sugar, and beat five minutes; two cups flour, and beat two minutes; one cup cold water, and beat one minute, the grated rind, and half the juice of a lemon; a little salt and two more cups flour, with two heaping teaspoons yeast powder, and beat another minute. Observe the time exactly, and bake in cup cake pans.

SNOW CAKE.—*Mrs. Gardner.*
VERY NICE WITH ICE CREAM.

Beat to a cream half cup of butter and two cups of powdered sugar; add one cup of sweet milk and whites of four eggs, whisked to a froth; sift two cups and a half of flour with a heaping teaspoon of cream tartar; add this alternately with the whites of eggs. Dissolve half a teaspoon of soda in a little boiling water, and stir in the last thing. Flavor with almond water. Bake in a moderate oven about three quarters of an hour.

ANGEL CAKE.—*Mrs. Sell.*

Three gills fine granulated sugar sifted three times, two gills flour sifted three times, add one teaspoon cream tartar and sift three times again; whites of eleven eggs beaten very lightly; add altogether lightly; one teaspoon almond extract. Bake in slow oven forty minutes. The pan in which it is baked must not be buttered, and should have three standards at the rim, and should be turned bottom upward as soon as removed from the oven. It will steam while cooling and come out readily.

Wm. K. Rowell, { Notary Public and Conveyancer, 458 Ninth Street, residence 410 Thirteenth St., First House East of Broadway, Oakland.

SILVER CAKE.—*Mrs. M. S. Root.*

The whites of four eggs, one cup sugar, one-half cup of milk, two cups of flour, one tablespoonful of butter, one teaspoonful of yeast powder.

GOLD CAKE.—*Miss Carrie Root.*

The yolks of four eggs, one-half cup sugar, one large cup flour, not quite one-half cup milk, one tablespoonful butter, one teaspoonful yeast powder.

COMPANY CAKE.—*Mrs. Everett.*

Sift two teaspoons yeast powder into three cups sifted flour; beat four eggs, add two cups fine sugar; now stir gradually into the eggs and sugar a half cup of cold water; next add lightly the prepared flour; last stir in one-half cup of melted butter. (Melt it over the teakettle, but do not allow it to get hot.) Put half the dough in a baking pan; then to the remainder add one-half teaspoonful each of cinnamon, cloves and nutmeg, and fill a second pan. Mind the rules for cake baking, and you will have two kinds of light and palatable cake. Try it. Frost it with the new frosting also quickly made.

BOILED ICING.

Two cups sugar, water enough to keep from burning; put on the stove to cook. When the sugar is melted and while hot, add the beaten whites of four eggs, spread on the cake while hot.

THE NEW FROSTING.—*Mrs. Buck.*

Take a teaspoonful of gelatine; cover with hot water and set it in a pan of hot water upon the stove until dissolved; let it cool and then stir in a cupful of powdered sugar. Flavor with almond.

FILLING FOR LAYER CAKE.—*Mrs. Gardner.*

Take one cup of sugar and a little water boiled together until it is brittle when dropped in cold water. Remove from the stove and stir quickly into it the well-beaten white of one egg. Add to this a cup of chopped hickorynut meat. Place between layers and over the top.

E. A. Brown, { Wholesale and Retail Dealer in Wood and Coal, 410 and 412 Ninth Street.

NUT CAKE.—*Miss Adelaide Elliott*

Make the cake the same as for jelly roll.

FILLING.

Three cups walnuts beaten fine, teaspoon of salt added, whites of five eggs whipped stiff, small cup of sugar. Mix well. Use as jelly. Yolks of eggs used in the cake.

ENGLISH WALNUT CAKE.—*Mrs. R. E. Cole.*

Make a nice cup cake and bake in jelly tins, three layers, half an inch thick. Two pounds English walnuts. Crack the nuts carefully, taking care to remove all bits of shell. Select the whole half meats that have the whitest skin for the top. Chop or break the remainder of the meats fine. Put a thin frosting between each layer of cake, and sprinkle thick with chopped meats. Make your frosting thicker for the top, and lay on your large pieces of walnut meat, half burying it in the frosting. You can blanch your meats by pouring over them boiling water, but it somewhat destroys the rich flavor of the nuts.

CAKE WITH ALMOND FILLING.—*Mrs. Niswander.*

Four eggs, three cups flour, two cups sugar, one cup milk, three-fourths cup butter, two teaspoons cream tartar, one teaspoon soda; beat eggs together, cream the butter and sugar, sift cream tartar into flour, dissolve soda in milk. Bake in eight thin layers.

FILLING.

Blanch and chop finely one pound almonds, mix with one teacup sugar, beaten yolks of two eggs, and one-half pint of thick sour cream. Lastly add whites, beaten to a thick froth, with vanilla to taste.

LEMON CAKE.—*Mrs. Craig.*

Make the filling first as follows: place the grated rind and juice of one large lemon in a tin cup with one teacup of white sugar. Set in a dish of boiling water on the fire, stirring occasionally until the sugar is dissolved. Then add the beaten yolk of one egg with a piece of butter the size of an egg, and stir until it thickens. Have ready the white of the egg beaten to a froth to be added last, and set the mixture aside to cool.

Get Your Stamping and Embroidery { Done at **MISS NAISMITH'S,** 1161 Broadway.

Make a cake of one cup of sugar, two tablespoons melted butter, three eggs, four tablespoons milk, a little salt, one and a half cups of flour, and two teaspoons yeast powder. This will make four sheets baked in jelly cake tins.

AMBROSIA JELLY FOR CAKE.—*Mrs. M. S. Root.*

One egg, one cup of sugar, three large apples grated, and one lemon (without the skin). Let it boil and spread between cake.

CHOCOLATE CAKE.—*Miss Lizzie Myrick.*

Two cups of sugar, one cup of butter, three and one-half cups of flour, five eggs, leaving out the whites of two; half cup of milk, half cup of water, two teaspoonfuls of yeast powder. Bake in one sheet or in layers.

Frosting.—Whites of two eggs, one and one-half cups of powdered sugar, six tablespoonfuls of grated chocolate, two teaspoonfuls of vanilla.

CHOCOLATE CAKE.—*Mrs. Craig.*

One cup butter, two cups sugar, five eggs, leaving out two whites, one small cup milk, three cups of flour, one teaspoon soda, two teaspoons cream tartar. Bake in two long pans. For the frosting beat the whites of two eggs to a stiff froth, one and one-half cups of sugar, two teaspoons of grated chocolate. The cake must be cold before the frosting is put on.

CHOCOLATE ECLAIRS.—*Mrs. Morse.*

Four eggs, the weight of the eggs in sugar, half their weight in flour, one-fourth teaspoonful soda, one-half teaspoonful cream tartar; bake in little tins.

CHOCOLATE ICING FOR ECLAIRS.

One-fourth cake chocolate, one-half cup sweet milk, one tablespoonful corn-starch, one teaspoonful vanilla. Boil until thick, then sweeten with powdered sugar, taking care to make it sweet enough.

COCOANUT CAKE.—*Miss Cara M. Fisher.*

Six eggs, reserve the whites of four for frosting; beat whites and yolks separately, three cups of sugar, small half cup of thick cream, one cup milk, one teaspoon soda, two teaspoons cream tartar, four cups of flour, bake in jelly-cake tins.

Filling.—Two and one-half cups sugar; add a little water and boil until on dipping into it a broom wisp, bent into a loop by holding the ends between the thumb and fingers, a web is formed, then remove from the fire; add the four beaten whites, beat till cold; pile the cakes with a layer of frosting with desiccated cocoanut sprinkled on it between them and over the whole.

If the above quantity of cake proves more than is needed for the loaf of cocoanut cake, add some flavoring extract, and make a plain loaf or make jelly cake with it.

LEMON CAKE.—*Mrs. Israel Knox.*

Small half cup of butter, one cup of sugar, two eggs, half cup of sweet milk, two and a half cups of flour, one and a half teaspoons yeast powder, bake in jelly tins, three layers.

Filling—Three-quarters of a cup of cold water, two heaping teaspoons corn starch, juice and rind of one lemon, three-quarters cup of sugar; boil all until clear, then add the well-beaten whites of two eggs into the hot mixture.

ORANGE CAKE.—*Mrs. Agard.*

One and one-half cups of sugar, two cups of flour, one-half cup of water, one teaspoon cream tartar, one-half teaspoon soda, yolks of five eggs, whites of three, salt, grated rind and juice of one orange. Bake in layers and spread each with a frosting made with the whites of two eggs, grated rind and juice of one orange, and sugar.

JELLY CAKE.—*Mrs. Buck.*

One cup sugar, one cup sweet milk, two cups of flour, one egg, two tablespoonfuls melted butter, two teaspoonfuls cream tartar, one teaspoonful soda. Beat the butter and sugar with two tablespoonfuls milk, add the egg well beaten, white and yolk separately, two yolks will do, dissolve the soda in milk, add gradually, stirring to a cream, sift cream tartar with flour. Flavor to taste; bake in a very quick oven, in papered tins.

Horace Davis' Flour at Fish & Co's, Eighth and Market.

JELLY ROLL.—*Mrs. Collins.*

Three eggs, one cup sugar, one cup flour, one heaping teaspoon yeast powder, six or eight teaspoons water, pinch of salt; bake in dripping-pan, lay on towel and roll.

JELLY FRUIT CAKE—*Mrs. Carpenter.*

Two cups of sugar, one cup of milk, three eggs, three cups flour, two-thirds cup butter, one teaspoon cream tartar, one-half teaspoon soda. Take two pans, and put one-half of the above mixture for the plain cake, and into the other half put one tablespoon of molasses, one large cup chopped raisins, one-fourth pound sliced citron, one teaspoon cinnamon, one-half teaspoon allspice, one-half nutmeg, one-fourth pound flour; bake each in two thin cakes, alternating the light with the dark, spreading jelly between.

HARLEM JUMBLES.—*Mrs. Dart.*

Three-quarters of a pound of butter, one pound of white sugar, one pound and a half of flour, three eggs.

NAHANT BUNS.—*Miss Perkins.*

Three cups of sweet milk, one cup each of yeast and sugar, flour enough for a stiff batter. Raise over night; in the morning add one cup each of sugar and buttter, one grated nutmeg, one teaspoonful of soda, enough flour to make it stiff like bread. Let it rise, then cut it like biscuits, and rise again. Bake in a hot oven.

PANCAKES.—*Mrs. Gardner.*

One cup of white sugar, two or three eggs, one-half pint of sweet milk, tablespoon of melted butter or lard, a little nutmeg and salt, one teaspoon of cream tartar, one-half teaspoon of soda; make the batter rather stiff, and drop from a spoon into hot lard and fry.

DOUGHNUTS.—*Mrs. Everett.*

Four cups of flour, one cup sifted sugar (brown), one cup sour milk, two eggs, one-half teaspoonful soda, one teaspoon each of cinnamon, clove and salt, and a piece of butter as large as an egg.

Swiss Confectionery, { Ladies' and Gentlemen's Ice Cream and Coffee Saloon, 416 Twelfth Street. Wm. J. F Laage, Prop.

Sift the soda, salt, and spice into the flour. Beat the eggs, stir in the sifted sugar, then add the butter (melted), and next the sour milk. Now add the prepared flour, (not by degrees), stir, and roll out.

DOUGHNUTS.—*Mrs. Dyer.*

Three eggs, two cups sugar, one cup milk, one teaspoon butter, two teaspoons yeast powder, a little salt, spice to taste, and enough flour to roll out.

(If the sugar is dissolved in warm milk, doughnuts will not absorb the fat in which they are cooked.)

CRULLERS.—*Mrs. Doe.*

One coffee cup of sugar, one coffee cup of cream, one egg, one nutmeg, two dessert spoonfuls of yeast powder, flour enough to roll, and cut not quite a fourth of an inch thick.

CRULLERS.—*Mrs. Agard.*

One cup sugar, butter the size of a Hickorynut, three eggs, one cup sweet milk, nutmeg, flour in which is sifted two heaping teaspoons baking powder.

CARAWAY COOKIES.—*Mrs. Craig.*

One cup sugar, three eggs, one cup butter, one teaspoon caraway seed, two teaspoonfuls baking powder, flour enough to roll out well.

(In all recipes which call for molasses, remember that New Orleans molasses is far preferable to syrup.)

GINGER CRACKERS.—*Mrs. Mary A. Knox.*

One cup molasses, one cup sugar, one-half cup butter, one-half cup hot water, one teaspoonful cream tartar or yeast powder, one-half teaspoonful soda, one tablespoonful ginger; make very stiff with flour, and roll thin.

GINGER BREAD.—*Mrs. Agard.*

One cup molasses, one-half cup butter, one teaspoon cream tartar in one cup cold water, two teaspoons soda, flour sufficient to make as thick as ordinary cake; spice with ginger or clove.

Gelatine and Ginger at Kelsey & Flint's.

OLD-FASHIONED SUGAR GINGER BREAD.—

Mrs. Agard.

One and one-half cups sugar, one cup butter, two eggs, two teaspoons ginger, one teaspoon soda dissolved in a little hot water, flour. Knead stiff, roll thin, bake quickly.

MOLASSES GINGER BREAD.—*Mrs. R. E. Cole.*

Two cups of best New Orleans molasses, one cup of thick sour cream, one teaspoonful soda, one egg, butter size of small egg. Rub your soda free from lumps and stir dry into your molasses, soften your butter so that it will easily mix in, add that with your well-beaten egg, also one-half teaspoon of allspice, one-half teaspoon cinnamon, one-fourth teaspoon of cloves, pinch of salt, enough flour to make as stiff as cup cake; the quantity of flour depends somewhat on the thickness of the cream. Bake in slow oven.

GINGER CAKE.—*Miss Ferry.*

One cup of molasses and one of sugar; one-half cup of butter, one egg, one teaspoon of soda, one cup of hot water, one teaspoon of cinnamon, one of ginger, and a very little salt.

ROCHESTER MOLASSES COOKIES.—*Mrs. Brewer.*

Three cups New Orleans molasses and two even tablespoonsful soda, stirred to a froth. Add three well beaten eggs, one cup lard, one teaspoon each of salt, ginger and cinnamon; stir thoroughly and mix very stiff with flour. Sift sugar over them after they are rolled, and bake in a quick oven.

CALOU & SCHEVANTON,

French Laundry,

1916 San Pablo Avenue,   **Oakland.**

The renovating of fine CLOTHS, BLANKETS, CURTAINS, FLANNELS and LACES a specialty.

No Machines Used.

LIGHT DESSERTS.

AMBROSIA.—*Mrs. Israel Knox.*
DELICIOUS.

Pare and cut in small pieces twelve oranges, pare and slice from two to six bananas, grate two cocoanuts; place first your oranges in a glass dish; sugar to taste; then put on the bananas and sugar, then the grated cocoanut and another sprinkle of sugar, and you have a delicious, as well as ornamental dessert. Your own taste will dictate the amount of sugar needed. Some leave out the bananas entirely.

CHOCOLATE BAVARIAN CREAM.—*Mrs. C. A. Grow.*

One pint of cream, one cupful of milk, one-half cup of sugar, one ounce of chocolate, half a package of gelatine; soak the gelatine in half of the milk, and whip the cream to stiff froth; scrape the chocolate and add two tablespoonfuls of sugar to it; put over the fire with one tablespoonful of hot water, stir until smooth and glassy; have the remaining half cup of milk boiling, stir the chocolate into it and add the gelatine; strain into a tin basin and add sugar; set in a pan of ice-water, and beat the mixture until it begins to thicken, then add the whipped cream, and when well mixed turn into a mold. Serve when hard with whipped cream.

CHARLOTTE RUSSE.—*Mrs. Israel Knox.*

One quart cream, whites of eight eggs; place the cream on ice for two or three hours; beat it well; beat eggs to a stiff froth; mix together, sweeten to taste, and flavor with vanilla.

Take one-half box Cox's gelatine, pour on a little cold water, and let it stand an hour; then pour on boiling water enough to dissolve and stir it into the cream. When about half set pour into the mold which must be lined with sponge cake.

SHERBET.—*Mrs. Flint.*

Rub rind of three lemons into eight ounces of sugar, one pint of cold water, the juice of three lemons and of two sweet oranges; two

---

Buy your Fish of Edwards Bros. 468 Eleventh St.

or three times this quantity may be used, and freeze the same as ice-cream.

ISINGLASS BLANC MANGE.

Two ounces of isinglass, three pints of milk, half a pound of sugar, lemon; boil five minutes.

SPANISH CREAM.—*Mrs. S. Woods.*

Soak one-half box of gelatine in enough cold water to cover, one hour; one pint of milk, let it come to a scald; yolks of four eggs, one small cup of sugar. Turn the gelatine into the milk and stir just enough to dissolve; pour some of the hot milk into eggs and sugar; then put all together and stir rapidly until it begins to thicken like custard; add whites well beaten, after removing from the fire; flavor and pour gently into mold. Serve with whipped cream or custard.

TAPIOCA CREAM.—*Mrs. Agard.*

One quart milk, three tablespoons tapioca, three eggs, one-half cup sugar, flavoring. Soak the tapioca over night in cold water; in the morning heat the milk and stir in the tapioca; when boiling, add yolks of eggs and sugar; when as thick as cream remove from the fire; when cool, flavor and spread with the whites of eggs whipped and sweetened.

PINK CREAM.—*Mrs. E. S. Cole.*

Whip one pint of thick sweet cream with one cupfull of currant jelly, sweeten and serve in jelly glasses. Currant, raspberry, or strawberry juice may be used in place of jelly.

BANANAS AND CREAM.—*Mrs. Agard.*

Peel and slice the fruit, and set on ice for a few hours; whip and sweeten the cream and spread over, or serve with the fruit, or sprinkle sugar over the fruit, and pour around it the cream unwhipped.

ORANGES FOR LUNCH.

Soak half a box of gelatine in a cup of cold water, when soft, add two teacups of boiling water, when entirely dissolved add one teacup

---

The wife and daughter of a prominent citizen assures us they feel that they cannot do without Kalliodont.

of sugar, the juice of six oranges and also of two lemons; strain this; have ready oranges prepared by cutting the part next to the stem, about one-third from the top of the orange; carefully remove the inside which may be used in making the jelly, fill with the jelly; replace the upper part and tie with a narrow ribbon.

STRAWBERRY ICE.—*Mrs. Agard.*

Four lemons, juice only, four cups sugar, four cups water, two pounds of strawberries, and one cup of sugar. Make a lemonade of the lemon juice, sugar and water; stand on ice. Mix the berries with one cup of sugar, and when the juice is somewhat extracted, mash the fruit smooth; add more sugar if desired. When ready to freeze, stir the strawberry into the lemonade and freeze as cream.

PEACH CUSTARD.—*Mrs. Abernethy.*

One can of peaches, three eggs, three cups milk, one-half cup sugar, two tablespoons corn starch, butter size of a walnut. Scald the milk, stir in corn starch, wet in cold milk, and cook till thick; take off the fire, beat in the sugar, butter and beaten yolks of the eggs, put in the white of one, whisk thoroughly. Drain the syrup from peaches, and cover the bottom of baking dish with them, and pour the mixture over. Bake in quick oven from ten to fifteen minutes, or till custard is set; then spread with a meringue of the whipped whites flavored with peach juice; brown on top; to be eaten cold.

OUR FAVORITE APPLE MERINGUE.
Mrs. Van Blarcom.

Half fill your dish with a rich apple sauce flavored with the rind of a lemon; make a boiled custard with the yolks of eggs only, and pour it over the apples. Make with the whites of the eggs, a meringue and pile it prettily over the custard. If your dish will bear the heat, set in the oven to brown a little. If in a glass dish and you have no "salamander," do as we do ours—brown with the fire shovel made hot.

ICE CREAM.—*Mrs. Israel Knox.*

Two quarts milk, half box Cox's gelatine soaked in a little cold milk, one quart of cream, one pint of sugar; flavoring to taste. Pour the boiling milk on the soaked gelatine, add the sugar; when this mixture is thoroughly cold, add the cream and flavoring and freeze. This makes one gallon when frozen.

ICE CREAM.—*Mrs. Buck.*

To one quart of milk add, while cold, one-half teaspoon of Sea Moss Farina, bring to a boil, stirring often; let it cook slowly thirty minutes. Set aside to cool. When cold whip one pint of sweet cream, and whisk all briskly for two or three minutes; sweeten and flavor to taste. Less cream will do.

ICE CREAM.—*Mrs. Niswander.*

One quart milk, three eggs, one pint cream, one coffee cup white sugar, one tablespoon vanilla, one tablespoon corn starch, slightly heaped; heat milk to boiling point; stir in sugar and corn starch; dissolve in a little cold milk; cook ten minutes; remove from stove, and add the well beaten eggs. Set away to cool. When ready to freeze, add the cream and vanilla. This makes three quarts when frozen,

TRIFLE.—*Mrs. Luke Doe.*

A layer of sponge cake in a dish. Make a soft custard, and flavor with vanilla. Blanch beforehand a cup of almonds, chop fine and soak them in a teaspoon of vanilla.

Directions for Mixing.—Pour the custard over the layer of cake, then sprinkle over it the nuts; then over that a layer of raspberry jam, or any other kind you may prefer; finally cover with whipped cream.

MACAROON PUDDING.—*Mrs. Bartlett.*

Take macaroon cakes, put them in a deep glass dish, pour over them warm soft custard. Beat the whites of eggs with or without currant jelly; take it up with a spoon and dot the cakes as they rise to the top closely with it. This is a very pretty dish for lunch.

COCOANUT AND CHOCOLATE BLANC MANGE.
Mrs. Van Blarcom.

One quart milk, four tablespoonfuls corn starch, let these boil together for at least fifteen minutes; when boiled beat in the whipped whites of two eggs. Divide the blanc mange. Into half of it stir the grated meat of a cocoanut. Into the other half grate (while still hot) two squares of chocolate. Pour one upon the other as in marble cake.

A DELICIOUS DESSERT.—*Mrs. Van Blarcom.*

Bake a sponge cake in a shallow tin, so that the cake will be about two inches thick when done. Over this pour some boiled custard. Just before serving slice peaches and put a layer over the cake; then beat the whites of the eggs to a stiff froth, with very little sugar, and put over the top. Use only the yolks of the eggs for your custard. If the peaches are out of season oranges may be used.

SWEET CREAM.—*Mrs. G. W. Hume.*

One quart of milk, four eggs, one box gelatine, one cup of sugar, a half pound of crystalized fruit. Soak gelatine three hours in one cup of water, then scald milk, sugar and gelatine together, divide in equal parts, into one put the beaten yolks and strain, when cool stir into this part one-half the beaten whites slowly, into the other half beat the remaining whites of eggs; line a form with the crystalized fruit, pour in alternately the cream; flavor with lemon and vanilla. To be made the day before, and to be eaten with custard.

Oakland Home Insurance Company,

Of Oakland,   California.

Cash Capital, - - - $200,000.00

Transacts a general Fire Insurance Business.
Agencies in all the principal localities on the Pacific Coast.

The only Fire Insurance Company incorporated on the Pacific Coast outside of San Francisco, and whose assets are not liable to sweeping conflagrations.

Head Office, 469 Ninth Street, Oakland, Cal.

JOHN P. JONES, *President*   WM. F. BLOOD, *Secretary.*
JOS. S. EMERY, *Vice-President.*   L. B. EDWARDS, *Gen'l Agent.*

For DELICACY OF FLAVOR AND GREAT STRENGTH

MERTEN MOFFITT & CO.'S
CONCENTRATED FLAVORING EXTRACTS

Are unrivaled. They are used and endorsed by nearly all the leading hotels on the Pacific Coast, and their popularity is attested by the fact that their sale is greater than that OF ALL OTHER Flavoring Extracts on the Pacific Coast combined.

---o---

MERTEN MOFFITT & CO.'S
SUPERIOR
CELERY SALT

Is one of the most agreeable condiments that can be used on the table. It possesses in a convenient and concentrated form the flavor of the Celery Plant, and is a delicious addition to Soups, Gravies, Stews, Salads, Cheese, etc., etc.

---o---

Every WELL ORDERED HOUSE SHOULD KEEP

MERTEN MOFFITT & CO.'S
FURNITURE REVIVER.

It both cleans and polishes the furniture at one operation with very little labor, and the most inexperienced person can use it. It DRIES QUICKLY and leaves no greasy or sticky surface. The largest furniture dealers and piano and sewing machine establishments use it. TRY IT!! Pint Bottles at 50 Cents per bottle.

---o---

MERTEN MOFFITT & CO'S
Non-Poisonous
SILVERING SOLUTION

Deposits a coat of pure silver on plated ware, saving the wear on the original plating. It is an excellent thing to clean and renew Harness, Mountings, Door Plates, Stair Roads, Wash Stand Fittings, etc., and for cleaning Solid Silver it has no equal. It is perfectly harmless to the hands and will not scratch the finest Plate. **Ask your Grocer for it!!**

C. R. HANSEN & CO.

Employment Agents,

110 Geary and 624 Clay Streets,

SAN FRANCISCO, CAL.

Furnish on Short Notice and Free of Charge

Good Clerks,	Also—
Stewards,	Housekeepers,
Bakers,	Cooks,
Waiters.	Laundresses,
Porters,	Waitresses.
Bell-Boys,	Chambermaids,
Dishwashers,	Nurses and Girls for all
Kitchen Help;	kinds of Housework, of all Nationalities.

ALSO,

Experienced Farm Foremen,	Coopers,
Farm Hands,	Wheelwrights,
Teamsters,	Foremen,
Blacksmiths,	Loggers,
Hay Pressers,	Timber-Fallers,
Harvest Hands,	Saw-Mill Crews,
Milkers,	Miners,
Wood Choppers,	Brickmoulders and Setters,
Butter or Cheese Makers,	Quarrymen,
Engineers,	Railroad Laborers and
Carpenters,	Laborers for all kinds of work in
Painters,	any number.

TELEPHONE No. 495.

110 Geary Street, { ***TRY US!!*** } 624 Clay St., S. F.

PASTRY AND PUDDINGS.

Pastry should be handled with the lightest of fingers. Use the knife with a quick stroke that the paste be not dragged, and in covering a pie, on no account pound or press the border together roughly.

The proportion commonly used is four cups of flour to one and a half cups of shortening (half lard, half butter). About a coffee cup of water will give this the right consistency (ice-water is best). This makes three pies.

Reserve one-half or more of the butter; chop the remainder of the shortening into the flour with a knife, add the water, mixing lightly and quickly; flour the board and rolling-pin, roll out, handling lightly; put the reserved butter in little pieces over the paste, sprinkle with flour, fold up the paste, and roll again. One light rolling and spreading, with proper handling, makes better and lighter crust than many "turns."

Be particular about the heat of the oven! If not hot enough, the paste will become soggy and dull; if too hot, it will become set and burn before it is done.

PUFF PASTE.—*Mrs. B.*

One quart flour, three-quarters cup butter, yolk of one egg; chop half the butter into the flour, stir the beaten egg into half a cup of ice water; mix, roll out thin, spread with one-third of the remaining butter, fold, roll again, and so on till the remaining butter is used up. Set in a cold place ten or fifteen minutes before using. Wet with beaten egg, while hot.

LEMOM PIE.—*Mrs. D. W. C. Gaskill*

One grated lemon, one cupful of boiling water, a heaping tablespoonful of corn starch, one cupful of sugar, butter size of an egg, two eggs, yolks and whites beaten separately; add the sugar and butter while boiling; remove from the stove, and add the eggs and lemon. When baked add the whites of the eggs with a little sugar; and return to the oven to brown.

Oakland Transfer Co. } San Francisco Office, 3 Post St. 28 Market St.

LEMON PIE.—*Mrs. Craig.*

The juice and yellow rind of one lomon, one cup sugar, one cnp of milk or cream, the yolks of three eggs, one tablespoonful of corn starch, and a pinch of salt; line a plate and bake the mixture, then beat the whites to a stiff froth, stir in lightly a spoonful of powdered sugar; spread on the pie and brown lightly.

LEMON PIE.—*Mrs. C. C. Wheeler.*

One lemon, one egg, one cup sugar, two apples grated, and one teaspoonful of cotn starch; bake with one crust; make a meringue for the top of the white of one egg and a teaspoonful of sugar; then brown.

LEMON TARTS.—*Mrs. Carpenter.*

One lemon, juice squeezed and rind grated, three eggs, one teacup sugar, two tablespoons melted butter; mix well and bake in small tins with good pastry.

RAISIN PIE.—*Mrs. W.*

Boil one pound chopped raisins covered with water one hour; let them cool, then add one chopped lemon, one cup of sugar, two tablespoons corn starch; add lemon juice last; bake between two crusts; this quantity will make three pies.

APPLE PIE—*Mrs. Collins.*

Cut in quarters nice tart apples, or if your apples are not tart use half a lime with them; line the plate with your crust, and before filling lay two tablespoons brown sugar on the bottom, with a light sprinkle of flour over it. Lay on your apples in rows around the plate, fitting them together smoothly; add a piece of butter the size of a walnut, a scatter of cinnamon and nutmeg, and a tablespoonful of water; cover with crust and bake.

CUSTARD PIE.

Three eggs to a pint of milk, two tablespoons sugar, a little salt. Beat yolks and whites separately, add milk, then the sugar; line a plate, fill and bake immediately.

Wm. K. Rowell, { Notary Public and Conveyancer, 458 Ninth Street, residence 410 Thirteenth St., First House East of Broadway, Oakland.

PASTRY AND PUDDINGS.

TRANSPARENT TARTS.—*Mrs. Collins.*

Line small oval fluted cake tins with paste, and put in filling made as follows:—

Four eggs, two cups sugar, three-fourths cup of butter; beat together as for cake. Add the juice of two oranges, one teaspoon each of lemon and vanilla. Bake about ten minutes.

COCOANUT TARTS.—*Mrs. E. S. Cole.*

Take one and one-half cups of sugar, a piece of butter the size of an egg, and braid them together; then four eggs and half a cup of sugar beaten to a froth; mix all together with a cup and a half of milk, then add six cups of grated cocoanut. Put into scalloped tins lined with a rich paste.

STRAWBERRY SHORT-CAKE.—*Miss Ella Glenn.*

One pint of flour, a piece of butter the size of an egg, and one and a half teaspoons of yeast powder; mix with milk as soft as you can knead, handle lightly, place in two round pans, bake quickly; split, butter, and fill plentifully with berries and sugar, cover with the other crust, put in the oven for a few minutes; serve. A little thick cream poured over the berries is an improvement.

SQUASH PIES.—*Mrs. Brewer.*

One pint squash, one quart milk, one cup sugar, three eggs, one tablespoonful butter, a little salt, a teaspoon of lemon extract. Strain the squash through a sieve, boil the milk with the salt and butter in it; mix the squash, sugar, and flavor, and pour on gradually the boiling milk, adding last the eggs well beaten, yolks and whites together. Have the pastry ready in the tins, and bake immediately in a quick oven. If the squash is not dry add to it three small crackers, rolled very fine.

MINCE PIES.—*Mrs. J. H. Brewer.*

Chop the meat, suet and apples separately, and measure the ingredients thus: three bowls of meat, three of apples, one of suet, one of citron cut small, two of raisins, two of currants, four of sugar, one of molasses, two of boiled cider, and one of some kind of syrup

---

Swiss Confectionery, { Ladies' and Gentlemen's Ice Cream and Coffee Saloon, 416 Twelfth Street. Wm. J. F Laage, Prop.

from fruit. (The vinegar left from sweet pickles will take the place of cider, and fruit syrup). Add powdered clove, nutmeg, cinnamon, and salt to suit the taste.

CREAM PIE.—*Mrs. N. B. Carpenter.*

Make the crust; after putting it on the plate, prick it (so that it will not raise up in blisters) and bake it. Put one pint of milk in a pan over a kettle of boiling water; beat well the yolks of two eggs, add a tablespoonful of corn starch dissolved in a little cold milk (reserved from the pint), one small cup of sugar; stir this into the boiling milk smoothly; when it thickens flavor with vanilla. Pour this into the well-baked crust; beat the whites, add two spoons of sugar, spread over the top, place in the oven to brown.

LEMON PUDDING.—*Mrs. Brewer.*

One quart of milk, four eggs, one pint bread crumbs, one cup of sugar, butter the size of an egg, one lemon; grate the rind of the lemon, beat the yolks of the eggs well, and mix with milk, crumbs, and sugar; put in buttered dish, and lay the butter in little bits on top. Bake a light brown; and when cold beat the whites of the eggs to a stiff froth, and add one-half cup sugar, and a little more than half the juice of the lemon. Spread over the pudding and brown in the oven.

BREAD PUDDING.—*Mrs. Agard.*

One quart hot milk, one pint bread crumbs dry and fine, four eggs, two tablespoons melted butter, one-fourth teaspoon soda in hot water, nutmeg. Stir the crumbs into the hot milk. Beat yolks of eggs very light and add with the butter nutmeg and soda. Last add the whipped whites. Bake and eat hot with lemon sauce.

ENGLISH PLUM PUDDING.—*Mrs. Craig.*

One pound bread crumbs; one-half pound leaf suet chopped fine; one pound raisins stoned, one pound currants, one-half pound *mixed* preserved citron, lemon and orange thinly sliced; one-half nutmeg grated; one teaspoon each of cinnamon, clove and salt; one large cup sugar; one cup flour; three teaspoons yeast powder, twelve eggs.

E. A. Brown, { Wholesale and Retail Dealer in Wood and Coal, 410 and 412 Ninth Street.

Place the mixture in a tin dish with a perfectly tight cover and set it in a large kettle that can also be covered close. Keep plenty of boiling water in the kettle, but not enough to boil over the top of the pudding-dish. Boil eight hours.

ENGLISH PLUM PUDDING.—*Mrs. Morse.*

Two cups flour, two cups of sugar, one cup of milk, one nutmeg, one teaspoonful salt, four teaspoonfuls baking powder, one-half pound currants, one-half pound stoned raisins, chopped fine, one-half pound suet chopped fine. Steam four hours.

Hard sauce—One cup sugar, one-half cup butter, four tablespoons currant jelly whipped to a cream.

ENGLISH PLUM PUDDING.—*Mrs. R. E. Cole.*

One cup molasses, one cup sweet milk, two cups suet, two cups raisins, two cups currants, one-half pound citron, one-half pound candied lemon peel, one-half teaspoon soda, one teaspoon cream tartar; salt well; all kinds of spice, flour enough to make stiff as fruit cake. Steam three hours.

SNOW PUDDING.—*Mrs. McLean.*

One-half box of gelatine, dissolved in one pint of water; add peel of two and juice of one lemon, two and one-half cups of sugar; strain, and when it begins to jelly, beat in thoroughly the whites of five eggs, previously well beaten, and put in the mold. With the yolks of eggs make a boiled custard and pour around the form just before serving.

CORN STARCH PUDDING.—*Mrs. Gardner.*

One pint of sweet milk, whites of three eggs, two tablespoons of corn starch and a little salt; put the milk in a dish and place in a kettle of hot water on the stove, and when it reaches the boiling point add the sugar, then the starch, dissolved in a little cold milk, and lastly the whites of the eggs whipped to a stiff froth. Beat it, and let cook a few minutes. Then pour into a mold. For sauce, make a boiled custard as follows: Bring to boiling point one pint of milk; add three tablespoons of sugar, then the beaten yolks, thinned by adding a little milk, stirring all the time until it thickens, but not so long as to curdle. Flavor with vanilla.

The Travelers { Is the only accident company that has a record.

PLAIN SUET PUDDING.—*Mrs. Agard.*

One cup chopped suet, one cup milk, two cups flour, one-half cup molasses, one cup raisins or currants, one small teaspoon soda, salt, cinnamon and nutmeg. Steam three hours; serve with sauce.

LEMON SAUCE FOR SUET PUDDING.

One-half cup sugar, very small piece of butter, stir to a cream; add one egg well beaten, and the juice of one-half of a lemon. Just before serving, add a little boiling water, stirring well.

OMELETTE PUDDING.—*Mrs. Abernethy.*

Four eggs beaten, whites and yolks separately, one cup milk, one slice bread, salt. Boil the milk, pour it over the crumbled bread, and beat it fine. Add beaten yolks of eggs, salt, and lastly the whites beaten stiff. Pour half the mixture in the hot buttered spider. When the bottom is brown, put the spider in a hot oven until the eggs set, lay slices of peaches sprinkled with sugar on one half, and turn the other over them. Eat hot. It does not hurt the first one to stand while the second is cooking. It is nice as an omelette, or with oysters or tomatoes instead of peaches.

BATTER PUDDING.—*Mrs. Green.*

Eight eggs, eight tablespoonful of flour, one quart of milk, bake in cups.

BAKED BATTER PUDDING.—*Mrs. Knox.*

WITH STRAWBERRY SAUCE.

Beat six eggs with eight heaping tablespoons of flour until smooth; stir this mixture thoroughly into one quart of fresh milk; salt to taste; strain into a buttered dish. Bake in a moderately quick oven one-half hour or until it rises and breaks open on the top; serve immediately. To be eaten with a sauce made of one cup of sugar, one-half cup butter beaten to a cream, and one-half cup strawberries stirred in.

FRUIT PUDDING.—*Miss Carrie Perkins.*

One cup molasses, one cup milk, one teaspoonful saleratus, two eggs, three cups flour, one-half cup melted butter, one cup raisins, one cup currants. Boil two hours.

Use Kelsey & Flint's Flavoring Extracts.

RICE PUDDING.—*Mrs. Everett.*

(Best ever made in spite of its being the cheapest.) One quart milk, two heaping tablespoonfuls rice, a piece of butter size of a walnut, and a little salt. Two tablespoonfuls of sugar. Bake in a slow oven two hours ; stir twice during the first hour. Eaten either hot or cold, with or without sauce. If you are using your oven this pudding can be cooked upon the back of the stove the first hour. Flavor with cinnamon.

CARROT PUDDING.—*Mrs. M. P. Downing.*

One cup of grated carrots, one cup of grated potatoes, one cup of suet, one cup of sugar, one cup of currants, two cups of flour, two tablespoonfuls of milk, sweet or sour; use soda if you have sour milk; yeast powder if sweet milk; use spices, cinnamon and cloves, also nutmeg. Steam in a pudding mold three hours.

COFFEE PUDDING.— *Mrs. M. E. Shaw.*

Sufficient coffee to moisten one quart of bread crumbs, one cup of brown sugar, one cup each of raisins, currants and citron, three eggs, one teaspoonful of soda, season with different spices and steam one hour. To be eaten with a good pudding sauce.

SWEET POTATO PUDDING.—*Mrs. Richards.*

Boil one quart of sweet potatoes very tender, rub them while hot through a colander, add six eggs, twelve ounces of powdered sugar, ten ounces of butter, nutmeg and lemon. Line the dish with a paste ; when baked sprinkle the top of the pudding over with sugar, and cover it with bits of citron.

QUEEN'S PUDDING.—*Mrs. Bartlett.*

One pint of bread crumbs to one quart of milk, one cup of sugar, the yolks of four eggs well beaten, the grated rind of one lemon, piece of butter the size of an egg. Bake until done but not watery, then whip the whites stiff, and beat in one cup of sugar, in which stir the juice of a lemon. Spread the pudding with any kind of preserves you prefer or currant jelly, pour the whites of the eggs over it, and return to the oven to brown, serve with cold cream.

Cure for Consumption, at Fish & Co's, Eighth and Market.

SNOW PUDDING.—*Mrs. Porter.*

Two tablespoonfuls of gelatine dissolved in a cup of boiling water, two cups of sugar, the juice of two lemons, the whites of two eggs beaten to a stiff froth. Mix all together and stir briskly three-quarters of an hour; set away in a glass dish to cool.

SAUCE FOR SNOW PUDDING.

Yolks of two eggs, three tablespoonfuls of sugar and one whole egg, one pint of milk, put in a pail and set in a kettle of boiling water until it begins to thicken.

INDIAN PUDDING.—*Mrs. W. F. Kelsey.*

One quart milk put on to boil, with a pinch of salt. Stir together five good (not heaping) tablespoonfuls of corn meal, one cup of syrup; add to boiling milk, stirring all the time. Cook until thick, butter a dish, turn pudding into it; when milk-warm add two well-beaten eggs; bake slowly for two or three hours.

SAUCES FOR PUDDINGS, ETC.

No. 1.

Cream sauce. Boil half a pint of cream, thicken very little; add a lump of butter as large as a walnut, half a cup of fine sugar. When cold, add one lemon, rind and juice, grated or sliced, or nutmeg.

No. 2.

Stir together one cup of butter and one cup of sugar, yolk of one egg, one teaspoonful of flour; slice a lemon, and put all into a bowl or pitcher, add half a pint of boiling water.

No. 3.

Beat equal quantities of white sugar and butter to a cream, adding a little grated nutmeg, and beat all well together; put in a cool place to harden before using.

No. 4.

Take one cup of mollasses, one cup of vinegar, half cup of butter; simmer together and flavor with nutmeg.

No. 5.

One cup sugar, one-half cup of butter, one tablespoonful flour, one cup boiling water. Flavor with lemon or vanilla.

Buy your Fish of Edwards Bros. 468 Eleventh St.

OYSTER SAUCE.—*Mrs. Brewer.*
FOR BOILED CHICKEN.

Small plump oysters three dozen; butter three ounces, flour one dessert spoonful; the oyster-liquor, milk or cream, quarter pint; a little salt, and cayenne. Strain the liquor into a sauce-pan, and put it, with the oysters in it, where it will heat slowly, but not boil. Then take out the oysters, and add to the liquor three ounces butter, smoothly mixed with the flour; stir without ceasing till it boils and is perfectly mixed, then add the milk or cream and stir till it boils again; add the salt and pepper, and then the oysters, and keep by the fire till thoroughly hot. Turn into a well heated tureen, and send *immediately* to the table.

DRAWN BUTTER. (FOR FISH, ETC.)

Mix well two teaspoonfuls of flour with two-thirds of a teacup of butter; stir this in five large spoonfuls of boiling water; stir till the whole boils up once and it is ready for use. Long boiling destroys the flavor of the butter.

EGG SAUCE.

Boil two or three eggs hard, cut them fine, and stir them into your drawn butter; if too thick, add a little cream or rich milk.

CRANBERRY SAUCE.—*Mrs. A. L. Stone.*

Three pints of cranberries, one and one-half pints sugar, one pint of cold water. Put all together in a porcelain kettle, boil eight minutes without stirring. Set it away in the kettle till next day.

NEWLAND & PUMYEA'S

LIVERY  STABLE,

Seventh Street, at Railroad Depot, Oakland.

This Stable is connected with the Telegraph and Telephone Wires. All orders promptly attended to. CARRIAGES IN ATTENDANCE ON ARRIVAL OF EVERY TRAIN. Ladies' Phætons, Buggies and Saddle Horses to let at all hours. Horses boarded by the Day, Week or Month on the most reasonable terms.

CONFECTIONERY.

ALMOND BREAD.—*Mrs. Stone.*

Beat stiff the whites of three eggs, add one-half pound of suga[r] and beat twenty minutes. Blanche and chop fine one-half pound o[f] almonds and roast them with two ounces of sugar until they are rich brown. Mix the beaten white of the egg and sugar with th[e] roasted almonds, and drop in small cakes upon well-buttered pan[,] allowing the mixture to spread in baking; bake in a slow oven.

CHOCOLATE CREAMS.—*Miss Annie Mason.*

Two cups of granulated sugar, and half a cup of cream. Bo[il] well five minutes, then put it into a bowl, flavor with vanilla, [if] desired, and stir till it is stiff enough to roll out into little balls wit[h] the hands. Break up four or five sections of chocolate, put the[m] into a bowl, and set it over the tea kettle until it becomes soft; the[n] add a very little water, stir it well and roll the cream drops in i[t.] Drop on wax paper.

MACAROONS.—*Miss Fli[nt].*

Whites of three eggs beaten to a stiff froth; [ad]d one-half poun[d] powdered sugar, one-half pound dessicated coc[oa]nut, one-half pi[nt] rolled and sifted cracker crumbs, and one teasp[oon]ful of extract o[f] bitter almonds. Drop on buttered papers in a d[rip]ing-pan, makin[g] little round cakes. These are a very good imit[at]ion of the mac[a]roons made of chopped almonds.

BUTTER SCOTCH.—*Miss Flint.*

One cup New Orleans molasses, one cup butter, two cups powdere[d] sugar, pinch of soda; boil until it just hardens when a little dropped in a cup of cold water. Pour out thin.

CARAMELS.—*Miss Flint.*

One cup of chocolate cut up fine, one cup molasses, one cu[p] cream or milk, two cups white sugar, butter as large as an egg. Bo[il] until hard, stirring all the time. Flavor with vanilla.

Mountain Ice Co. { Office and Depot, 515 Fourth St., Oakland. Ice delivered [to] all parts of Oakland and Brooklyn. S. D. Smith, Manage[r.]

OLD-FASHIONED MOLASSES CANDY.
Miss Wheeler.

Syrup will not make good molasses candy; take one quart New Orleans molasses, boil until it crackles when dropped in cold water; just before taking up stir into it a level teaspoonful of baking soda; pour on plates and when cool enough to handle, pull.

KISSES.—*Miss Williams.*

Beat the whites of four eggs fifteen minutes, add one cup of sugar and one-half teaspoonful vanilla, and beat all together fifteen minutes more. Bake in a very slow oven three-quarters of an hour.

UNCOOKED CREAM CANDY.—*Miss Carrie Root.*

Take two pounds of confectioner's finest powdered sugar, put the white of one egg in a glass, beat enough to make it light, bnt not to an entire froth. In another glass measure the same amount of water and mix with the egg. Place the sugar on a slab or moulding-board; leave a little dry to mould with, make a hole in the center and pour in and mix with the sugar until it is the consistence of soft dough, and can be kneaded like dough, adding, if necessary, water enough to do so. Flavor with vanilla, then mold into any desired form, add nut meats or a coating of chocolate.

WHY WASTE

Your time, sugar and patience in attempting to make Candy, when you can buy the purest and best in the market of

GEORGE HAAS,

MANUFACTURER OF

Home-Made, Plain and Fine Candies,

824 MARKET STREET,

Phelan's Building,   SAN FRANCISCO.

☛ Candies forwarded by mail or express C. O. D. to any part of the country.

PRESERVED FRUITS.

Jams of all berry fruits are made by scalding and n fruit as for jelly, then adding a pound of sugar to a pou weighing the latter after it is prepared. and boiling unt becomes thick and smooth. Boil the fruit in its own ju tiful, for half an hour before adding the sugar. A half boiling will be enough. Too long boiling makes the frui dark.

For preserves allow pound for pound as for jam. clear syrup, use a gill of water to a pound of sugar. just on the boil, as the boiling point is when the scum c surface, yet once having boiled, the scum is broken syrup is never so clear.

CANNED FRUITS.—*Mrs. Wright.*

Select the best fruit; Pare and cut in halves; then ex cans, see that the tops all fit, and that none leak; or if y jars, see that the rubbers fit, and that the tops are ready. hot water, and let them stand until needed. Weigh frui allowing one-third of a pound of sugar to one pound of fr and apricots need more sugar. Put a little water in your put in the sugar, stirring constantly until it is dissolved. it boils up put in the fruit, as soon as this boils up fi picking out the softest first wtih a fork. When two-th fruit, pour in the juice through a strainer. Have ready pieces of cloth the size of a jar, wet in alcohol, and pi the fruit. This will collect the mould if any should fo seal as quickly as possible. If you use cans, look them you are through, to be sure there are no bubbles in the w use glass jars, screw them down again and again wh When filling your glass jars always place them on a v prevent their cracking. Have your fruit boiling hot all th fill very full to exclude the air.

FRUIT JELLIES.—*Mrs. Wright.*

Put your fruit into earthen dishes, and set them in kett

Dr. Merriman's { Fragrant Kalliodont, Beautifies, Preserves th Charms all who use it.

water, cover closely; heat the fruit until it is broken; then squeeze through a bag, or if you want it especially clear, tie it in a bag, and hang it up where it can drip over night. Measure your juice, and weigh your sugar, allowing three-fourths of a pound of sugar to one pint of juice. Put the sugar in tin dishes, and place in the oven to heat, stirring occasionally. Put the juice in a kettle over the fire, and let it boil from five to ten minutes, then stir in the sugar, which should be so hot that it will hiss as you stir it into the boiling juice; allow this to just boil up thoroughly, no more, as the longer it boils the darker it becomes; take off the fire, and fill the jelly glasses, which have been previously dipped in hot water. If the glasses are placed on a wet cloth while being filled they will not crack. When the jelly is firm, lay a piece of tissue paper, dipped in alcohol or brandy, on top of the jelly. Paste paper over the glass, and put away in a dry, dark place.

CURRANT JELLIES.

To five pounds of currants add one pound raspberries It improves the flavor.

Strawberries, apricots or peaches can be made to jelly by taking one-third the quantity of apple juice, adding to the other syrup and then proceeding as in other jellies.

CURRANT JELLY.—*Mrs. Wheeler.*

Ten pounds currants, eight pounds sugar; stem the currants and cook with sugar twenty minutes; dip out two quarts juice and put through a jelly bag and fill your glasses. Can the rest.

RASPBERRY OR BLACKBERRY JAM.—*Mrs. Wheeler.*

To twelve pounds of berries, take four pounds of tart apples peeled and quartered (the red Astrican and June), cook the fruit all together with just sufficient water in the beginning to keep the apples from scorching; boil hard for two hours; then twelve pounds of white sugar and boil hard twenty minutes. This is an English recipe and is very good.

APPLE JELLY.—*Mrs. A. T. Earl.*

Take red Astrican apples, and without paring, cut them up cores and all. Fill your *porcelain* kettle up to an inch or so of the brim

---

Do Not Go { To San Francisco for What you can get at **MISS NAISMITH'S,** 1161 Broadway.

with the fruit and pour in water until you cover it. Then let the fruit get well cooked before straining through a jelly bag. Return the juice to the kettle to be boiled till it looks clear and transparent. Then measure it, allowing for every bowl one bowl of crushed sugar, warmed in the oven, and boil briskly fifteen minutes. The jelly is then fit for the glasses.

If you wish to color and flavor the jelly, when the juice is returned to the kettle and before it is sweetened, put in for every two quarts of juice one pound of raspberries contained in a thin bag.*

* In preparing the jelly use no tin or iron utensils.

LEMON JELLY.—*Mrs. J. T. Agard.*

Four lemons, two ounces gelatine, one pound sugar, one quart boiling water; soak the gelatine in cold water till soft; add the juice and pulp of the lemons, and sugar; pour on the boiling water, and stir until all is dissolved. Strain into molds and set it by over night till jellied.

FIG MARMALADE.—*Mrs. Lacy.*

Three pounds of figs, two oranges, two lemons, two pounds sugar. Use pulp of the oranges, pulp and rind of the lemons; chop figs and all together; cook twenty minutes.

PRESERVED FIGS.—*Miss Perkins.*

One-half pound sugar to one pound fruit. Scrape green ginger, one small root being enough for seven or eight pounds of fruit, cut fine and boil with syrup; after it has flavored the syrup skim it out.

SPICED BLACKBERRIES.—*Mrs. Wright.*

To seven pounds fruit, use three pounds sugar and one pint vinegar. If the vinegar is very sharp use part water. Make as many little bags of thin cloth as you will have jars of fruit, allowing nearly two and one-half pounds to a quart jar. Put into each bag one teaspoon each of cloves, allspice, cinnamon, and mace; tie the bags up loosely. Make a syrup with the sugar and vinegar, and put in the bags of spices. When boiling put in the fruit and boil one hour. Seal as you would canned fruit.

Miss E. S. Buell, Decorative Art Rooms. Fancy Work of all Kinds.
1118 Washington Street, Oakland.

PRESERVED FRUITS. 73

SPICED PEACHES.

To nine pounds of peaches add four and a half pound of sugar, a pint of good vinegar, with whole cloves and cinnamon. Pare and halve the peaches and put in stone jar. Boil the vinegar, spices and sugar together a few moments and pour over peaches. Cover and let stand over night. In morning put all together in kettle and boil ten minutes.

If you wish for good success in making jellies, jams, and in canning fruits, always select fruit *ripe and fresh*, which can be obtained at

PORTER BROTHERS',

460 and 462 Eleventh St., bet. Broadway and Washington.

PAGE & AGARD,

DEALERS IN

Choice Family Groceries,

464 ELEVENTH STREET,

Between Broadway and Washington,   OAKLAND, CAL.

---o---

KEEP IN STOCK:

Horace Davis' Roller Mills Flour,	Rice Flour,	Tapioca,
Graham Flour,	White Corn Meal,	Sago,
Graham Meal,	Yellow Corn Meal,	Eastern Oat Meal,
Glutina,	Farina,	Oat Groats,
Granula,	Cracked Wheat,	Large Hominy,
Rye Flour,	American Cereals,	Small Hominy,
Rye Meal,	Crushed Indian,	Pearl Hominy.
	Corn Starch,	

Whether You Travel or not, Insure against Accidents in The Tavelers.

PICKLES AND CATSUPS

PICKLED PEACHES.—*Mrs. Wright.*

Pare the peaches, put one whole clove into each peach; pack them into a stone jar; make a syrup of three pounds sugar, one pint good cider vinegar to every eight pounds of fruit, one tablespoon whole allspice, and two tablespoons of acacia buds. Boil the syrup and spices about ten minutes, and pour over the fruit; put a plate on top of the fruit to hold it down. Let this stand twenty-four hours then pour off the syrup into the preserving kettle; when it boils put in the fruit and boil it until it begins to be soft, then put the fruit in your glass jars, and fill up with the syrup; put a small round cloth on top, as in canned fruit, and seal quickly.

RIPE CUCUMBER PICKLE.—*Mrs. McLean.*

Pare, core, and cut lengthwise, boil in vinegar and sugar; about one pound of sugar to one quart of vinegar; boil until clear and transparent. Skim and put in a jar while hot; add a few sticks of cinnamon. They should stand in salt and water over night after cutting, before cooking.

FIG PICKLES.—*Mrs. Lacy.*

Seven pounds of figs, three pounds of sugar, one-half pint vinegar two lemons sliced, cinnamon and cloves. Boil all together two hours, slowly.

GREEN TOMATO SWEET PICKLE.—*Mrs. Niswander.*

One fruit basket of green tomatoes, slice medium thickness sprinkle with one teacup of salt, and drain for twenty-four hours on sieve or colander; boil in two quarts of water to one of vinegar, for twenty-five minutes; drain again, and mix evenly with six very large sliced onions, two pounds brown sugar, one-half pound white mustard seed, two even tablespoons each of allspice, cloves, ginger mustard, cinnamon, one-half tablespoon cayenne pepper, and three quarts vinegar. Boil for twenty minutes. (The spice is not put in bags).

Cure for Consumption, at Fish & Co's, Eighth and Market.

CUCUMBER PICKLES.—*Mrs. Brewer.*

To each hundred cucumbers take a pint of salt, and pour on boiling water enough to cover them; cover tightly to prevent the steam escaping, and let them stand twenty-four hours. They are then to be taken out and wiped perfectly dry, taking care not to break the skin; place them in a jar in which they are to be kept, putting in occasionally a long, green paper; boil cider vinegar sufficient to cover them, adding cloves, allspice, and a little sugar: pour over the pickles, and cover tightly. In ten days to two weeks delicious pickles will be produced.

MIXED PICKLES.—*Mrs. Niswander.*

One fruit basket of green tomatoes, one small head cabbage, eight large onions, two large heads celery, three large green peppers, one-half pound white mustard seed. Chop tomatoes very fine, sprinkle over with one teacup salt, and hang up to drain for twenty-four hours; add other ingredients, chopped equally fine, and salted to taste; cover well with vinegar, and boil until partly cooked.

PICKLES.—*Mrs. Green.*

Slice green tomatoes, cucumbers and onions (of latter one-third quantity); soak cucumbers over night in salt and water; cook tomatoes in salt and water. Place horseradish in bottom of jar, then cucumbers, then tomatoes, and then onions, in layers with white mustard seed between. Pour all over hot vinegar and sugar.

PICKLES.—*Mrs. S. H. Covert.*

To one hundred small cucumbers, one quart of small onions sliced very thin, one-half teacup of salt sprinkled in layers, put in a colander under a heavy weight; after remaining six hours, drain, then add one gill sweet oil, one-half ounce of celery seed, one dessertspoon black ground pepper, one teaspoon black mustard seed; mix well and cover with cold cider vinegar. Put away in earthen jars.

CHOW CHOW.—*Mrs. D. W. C. Gaskell.*

One peck green tomatoes, nine large white onions sliced and sprinkled with a little salt; cover up in an earthen dish; let it stand all night, drain and rinse; then cover with vinegar, add one teacupful whole mustard seed, allspice, cinnamon, ground mustard, black pepper, red pepper to taste; one pint brown sugar; cook all slowly four or five hours.

PICCALILLI.—*Mrs. E. B. Thompson.*

To one peck green tomatoes sliced, add a pint of salt; cover with water and let them stand twelve hours; squeeze them out and let them remain in fresh water a few hours. Take ten or twelve green peppers and seven large onions, put them with the tomatoes and chop all fine; put them in a porcelain kettle with weak vinegar, and let them boil or scald a while; draw off the vinegar and take some good old cider vinegar, a pint of white mustard seed, and some grated horseradish, add two tablespoons brown sugar, mace, cinnamon, cloves, to your taste, and a small piece of alum; pour on the tomatoes and cover close.

PICCALILLI.—*Mrs. Wheeler.*

One gallon finely-chopped cabbage, one-half gallon green tomatoes, one quart green onions, one pint green peppers with seeds taken out; sprinkle salt over and let them remain over night. In the morning squeeze out the water, add four tablespoons ground mustard, two of cinnamon, two of ginger, two of celery seed, one of cloves, two pounds brown sugar, one-half gallon cider vinegar, and simmer twenty minutes. Put away in stone jars.

GRAPE CATSUP.—*Mrs. Carpenter.*

Take five pounds of grapes, boil and run through a colander; add two and one-half pounds of sugar, one pint vinegar, one tablespoon each of cinnamon, cloves, allspice, pepper, and one-half tablespoonful salt; boil until the catsup is a little thick.

PLUM CATSUP.—*Mrs. W. Wheeler.*

Seven pounds of plums, four pounds of sugar, one quart of vinegar, one tablespoon each of cinnamon, allspice, mustard, ginger, one-half tablespoon cloves, salt; cook plums a little, then put through a colander; add other ingredients, and boil slowly three hours.

CHILE SAUCE.—*Mrs. Everett.*

Twelve large ripe tomatoes, pared; two large onions, four long

---

Swiss Confectionery, { Ladies' and Gentlemen's Ice Cream and Coffee Saloon, 416 Twelfth Street. Wm. J. F. Laage, Prop.

green peppers, four tablespoons sugar, two cups vinegar, one tablespoon salt. Chop the onions and peppers fine, and place all together in a preserving kettle; simmer about three hours. Before adding the tomatoes dip out one cupful of the juice. Seal in gem jars.

CHILE SAUCE.—*Mrs. Howell.*

Forty-eight ripe tomatoes, eight green bell peppers, eight large onions, eight teacups of vinegar, four teacups brown sugar, eight teaspoons each of ginger, cinnamon, allspice, cloves, eight tablespoons of salt, one-half bottle Worcestershire sauce. Peel the tomatoes, chop the onions and peppers and boil together four hours; then add the other ingredients, and simmer long enough to get thoroughly mixed. Seal air tight.

REINHART'S BAZAAR
AND
CROCKERY STORE.

CROCKERY,
    GLASSWARE,
        VASES,
            PLATED WARE,
                BRIC A BRAC,
                    NOTIONS,
                        LEATHER WARE,
                          TOYS,
                              ETC., ETC., ETC.

REINHART & CO.

1105 BROADWAY,   OAKLAND.

Lessons in all kinds of Embroidery at Miss Naismith's, 1161 Broadway.

Patent Kitchen Cabinet!
OR "A PANTRY IN A NUT SHELL."

The above Cut represents our Kitchen Cabinet and Table combined.

The top is the size of an ordinary kitchen table; No. 6 is a kneading board for bread and pastry; No. 5 is a drawer the length of the table, divided into compartments for knives, forks, spoons, etc.; No. 4 is a drawer with two apartments, which will hold 10 lbs. in each division; No. 3 is a carving board for meats, etc., which can be laid flat on the top of the table, the same as the bread board; No. 2 is a drawer which will hold a 25-lb. sack of meal or rice; No. 7 is a large, deep drawer, which swings on hinges and will hold a 50-lb. sack of flour, and No. 1 is a small drawer, which is used for a scouring board, and has a compartment for the scouring brick.

Heretofore having been unable to fill all the orders constantly received from all parts of the State, I have increased my facilities for the manufacture of this Kitchen Cabinet, so that I may be prepared to supply my customers and the trade in general. The price is within the reach of all, $10.

ALL ORDERS PROMPTLY ATTENDED TO.

CHR. SCHREIBER, 1064 and 1070 Broadway, Oakland.

A Chapter for Dyspeptics.

"We never regret having eaten too little."—THOMAS JEFFERSON.

(These recipes have been prepared with the utmost care; many of them have been contributed by those who have practically tested them, and others have been selected from reliable sources).

UNLEAVENED BREAD.

Take Graham, rye, or oatmeal, add a very little salt, and water enough to make a batter as for griddle cakes; beat and work it, the more the better; have your oven hissing hot; make a thin loaf about a quarter of an inch thick.

GRAHAM BREAD.

Three quarts Graham flour, dissolve a little compressed yeast, add to it three pints milk and warm water, one teaspoon salt, half cup molasses, one teacup fine flour; stir together until thoroughly mixed; then let it rise until quite light and put into two good-sized pans; when light, bake thoroughly.

GRAHAM GEMS.

Take a quart or more of Graham flour, stir in water; make a batter a trifle thicker than griddle cakes, a pinch of salt, then stir briskly for a few minutes; have the gem-pans hot on the stove; put your batter into the oven so hot that it will raise them immediately. The lightness depends upon the heat of the oven.

WHITE GEMS.

Stir into warm milk, or cream and milk, white flour until it is of the right consistency to drop from the spoon. Just as it is ready for the oven beat in briskly the whites of two eggs, whipped to a stiff froth. Bake briskly. Good, wholesome cake is made by adding sugar and chopped raisins. These gems are light, brown, and crispy, and compared with the old-time, dyspeptic-provoking, saleratus biscuits, are infinitely superior both on the score of taste and health.

E. A. Brown, { Wholesale and Retail Dealer in Wood and Coal, 410 and 412 Ninth Street.

BEATEN BISCUIT.

One quart Graham flour, one teaspoon salt, mix stiff with water, beat with a rolling pin twenty minutes, and bake in a hot oven.

GRAHAM CRACKERS.

Two-thirds quart of Graham flour, one-third oat meal, one half teaspoon salt, one tablespoonful brown sugar; mix with boiling hot water, and knead until cool. Roll about an inch thick, prick with a fork and bake in a hot oven.

RYE OR INDIAN DROP CAKES.

Mix together two parts rye meal and one part Indian with cold water, until it is stiff enough to be easily stirred with a spoon; stir until it becomes creamy, which with a strong hand will require ten or fifteen minutes. Drop into hot gem pans, filling them full and bake in a moderately heated oven thirty or forty minutes. These are excellent cakes.

OLD-FASHIONED JOHNNY CAKE.

Put Indian meal in a pan and stir in boiling milk, making rather a stiff mixture; put this into baking tins, heaping up a little more than level full; bake in a hot oven, or it may be baked on a hot griddle on the top of the stove for half an hour, taking care it does not cook too fast. Turn once.

GRAHAM MUSH.

The standard, every day pudding. Stir slowly into fast boiling water, sprinkled from the hand, sufficient Graham flour to make a thin pudding; let it boil ten minutes and it is done.

CRACKED WHEAT.

Take clean, fresh-cracked wheat, one quart wheat to five quarts of water; boil in a double boiler moderately four or five hours.

Hasty pudding, oat meal pudding, rye pudding, and farina pudding, are all made the same as Graham except that oat meal should be cooked half an hour.

HOMINY.

Soak over night, and boil in a double boiler six hours.

The Travelers Is the oldest Accident Company in America; the largest in the world.

BOILED RICE.

Examine, and wash rice previous to cooking. Take one cup of rice to six cups of milk; set in a covered tin pail in a kettle of boiling water, and cook from two to three hours; stir occasionally.

SCOTCH PUDDING.

One teacup rich milk, two well-beaten eggs, and Graham flour to make a batter so stiff that it may spread with a spoon; three pints nice cooking apples, quartered and cut in two transversely, and laid in the pudding dish, sprinkle in enough sugar to sweeten agreeably, and flour enough to thicken the juice; then spread the batter over the top; bake moderately until the apple is done; cover the top with a paper if there is any danger of scorching.

OAT MEAL BLANC MANGE.

A delicious blanc mange may be made by stirring two heaping tablespoonfuls fine oat meal into a little cold water and then stirring in a quart of boiling milk; boil a few minutes, flavor, turn into a mold; when cold, eat with jelly and cream.

INDIAN PUDDING

One cup corn meal, one-half cup flour, mix with cold milk; stir in one quart boiling milk, remove from the fire and add one cup syrup, one-half cup sugar, one teaspoonful cinnamon, one teaspoonful salt, six to twelve apples, according to the size (pared and quartered), add one pint cold milk; bake in a moderate oven two hours.

GRANULA PUDDING.

Granula is one of the most palatable, healthful, and nutritious articles of diet in the world. One coffee cup granula, two eggs, three tablespoons sugar, three pints of milk; boil the milk and add it hot to the granula; soak until cool, then add sugar and the yolks of eggs; beat and stir in whites of eggs just before baking; bake in a slow oven one hour.

SIMPLE FRUIT SHORT-CAKE.

Roll out a dough made of two-thirds Graham flour, and one-third Indian meal mixed with thin cream, either sweet or sour, for shorten-

Get your Baking Powder of Kelsey & Flint.

ing. Bake on plates or pans, making the cakes less than an inch thick. Cut open and place between the two, mashed strawberries, blackberries, raspberries, or even apple sauce sweetened to taste.

PIE CRUST.

The easiest pie crust to make, and an excellent one, is composed of flour or meal wet up with cream and a pinch of salt.

No. 2. Stir into Graham flour boiling water to make a stiff dough. Do not knead, it makes it tough. The under crust should be rather thick and the upper thin, and the quicker it is baked the better. The fruit should be stewed or steamed before baking.

No. 3. Equal quantities corn starch and Graham flour wet with new milk makes a nice tender crust.

CORN SOUP.

Grate or cut off corn of six ears; put corn and cob in little more than one quart of water; boil twenty minutes, remove the cobs, add little more than one pint of milk; boil five minutes, then add piece of butter size of an egg; stir in thoroughly two well-beaten eggs just before taking up.

RICE SOUP.

Boil a soup bone of bits of meats left from a roast, for several hours. Cool, and skim off all the grease; strain through a sieve and add one cup of rice to two quarts of liquid; cook until the rice is soft. If the soup is thin, beat up an egg in one-half cup of cream and add just before serving.

MUTTON TOAST.

Cut in pieces one pound of mutton, the bony part is the best, and put on the stove early, in one quart of cold water. Cook slowly; when the meat is tender, strain the broth through a sieve and set away to cool. After removing the grease that has risen to the top, let the broth come to boiling, and add flour thickening with a little cream or butter. Meanwhile toast slices of white or brown bread, and dip in hot water to soften; pour the stew over the bread, adding the pieces of mutton, and you have a simple, wholesome, palatable, dish.

A FEW FAVORITE DIETETIC APHORISMS.

An hour of exercise to every pound of food. We are not nour-

Try Fish & Co's Block Butter, Eighth and Market.

ishod by what we eat, but by what we digest. Every hour you steal from digestion will be reclaimed by indigestion. He who controls his appetite in regard to the quality of his food, may safely indulge it in regard to the quantity. The oftener you eat the oftener you will repent it. Dyspepsia is a poor pedestrian; walk at the rate of four miles an hour, and you will soon leave her behind.

KOUMISS, WHAT IS IT?

TRADE MARK

KOUMISS is a white, creamy fluid, prepared from pure, fresh cow's milk, and possessing all its nutritive qualities, but in a form more easily assimilable. By its peculiar mode of preparation much of the preliminary work of digestion is performed.

EDWIN M. HALE, M. D., Professor of Materia Medica and Therapeutics, Chicago Medical College, says:

"As a medical man, I believe KOUMISS is almost a nutritive panacea for that class of diseases characterized by failure of nutrition from mal-assimilation. It will remain upon the delicate stomach when nothing else will, and will supply the body with nutriment when all other foods fail. I know no medicine so efficient for sleeplessness, when arising from nervous irritation, debility, or deficient supply of blood in the brain. A goblet full taken at bed-time, and possibly another in the night, causes calm and refreshing sleep, leaving no malaise, or headache, or loss of appetite in the morning. In fact, in sickness or in health, I know of no beverage so well adapted to our comfort as KOUMISS. I have known many little children given up to wasting diseases rapidly recover on the use of one bottle per day."

CHARLES W. KNOX, PROPRIETOR,
533 Knox Place, Oakland.

—o—

REDINGTON & CO., Wholesale Agents, 529 and 531 Market Street, San Francisco.

H. BOWMAN, Agent, Corner Ninth and Broadway, Oakland.

Arabian Coffee Mills!
No. 12 FOURTH STREET,
SAN FRANCISCO.

We have the most improved machinery for roasting and grinding; employ none but experienced hands, and using the best green Coffees that come to this market, are prepared to furnish Hotels, Restaurants, and parties using large quantities of Coffee, a superior article at minimum price.

This is the only place in the city where families can obtain their Coffee direct from first hands, and consequently they can get from us better Coffee for less money than at any other house.

We have all the various kinds of green Coffee, and our roasted and prepared Coffees range in price

From 12½ Cents to 45 Cents per lb.

We call special attention to our

ARABIAN ROAST.

It is a blending of selected Old Government Java and genuine Mocha Coffee. It is carefully roasted and glazed with pure white sugar, thus retaining its essential oil, great strength and rich aroma, which are so absolutely necessarily in a perfect Coffee. We make a speciality of this Coffee and know it to be the best in California. Any one who desires a fine Coffee should not fail to give it a trial.

We sell it 3 lbs. for One Dollar.

Our SPICES are strictly pure and are packed in full weight cans.

TEAS.

Our Teas are carefully selected for their superior drinking qualities and are all new crop, comprising all varieties and varying in price (in bulk) from 15 Cents to $1.50 per lb. Also, packed in 5 and 10 lb. boxes and 30 to 60 lb. chests. Families in the country will find it greatly to their advantage to obtain their Coffee, Tea and Spices direct from us, as aside from getting fresh goods they will effect a saving of about 20 per cent. *Samples sent free by mail.*

HILLS BROS'
No. 12 Fourth Street and Stalls 24 and 25 Bay City Market,
SAN FRANCISCO, CAL.

DRINKS.

TEA.—*Mrs. Knox.*

The bane of tea in many households is unboiled water, which can never extract the flavor it should. Be sure, then, that the water boils; put in your pot a teaspoonful of tea for each person, with one thrown in for a possible guest. Warm both tea and pot, then cover well with boiling water. Let this stand ten minutes (no longer) where it will keep *very hot;* this is *steeping*—the process always required before the larger quantity of water is added. It may just come to a boil, but boiling or too long steeping will give the *Japan* tea an "herby" flavor. Fill with boiling water and send to the table hot. the Oolong teas may steep one hour and a half without injury.

COFFEE.—*Mrs. Knox.*

In making coffee great care must be exercised in selecting the brand. I have found Hill's Bros. "Arabian Roast" to give the best satisfaction. It is what it pretends to be—a blending of "Old Government Java and "Genuine Mocha."

Stir a beaten egg into two teacups of ground coffee, cover with a pint of cold water and set upon the stove until it boils. Then pour a quart of boiling water into it and let it stand where it will keep at the boiling point five minutes. Pour a half cupful from the spout to remove the grounds and it is ready to serve. Long boiling makes coffee strong but not agreeable. If you cannot have cream to send to the table use rich boiled milk, which gives coffee a pleasant flavor. Keep your coffee pot clean and dry. A musty pot will spoil the flavor of the best made coffee. When eggs are dear a well-cleansed bit of dried fish skin can be used instead of an egg.

CHOCOLATE.—*Mrs. Knox.*

An ounce of chocolate for one person; scrape and boil it from five to ten minutes, with about four tablespoons of water; when it is very smooth, add a pint of new milk, boil, stir it well and serve; if you wish to make it of water, use nearly a pint of water, instead of milk, and send rich cream to the table with it.

Mountain Ice Co. { Office and Depot, 515 Fourth St., Oakland. Ice delivered to all parts of Oakland and Brooklyn. S. D. Smith, Manager.

COCOA.

Boil two large spoonfuls of ground cocoa in a quart of water half an hour; pour in three gills of milk, and boil it up again; skim off the oil if too rich.

REFRESHING DRINK FOR THE SICK.—*Mrs. McLean.*

Raspberry vinegar or shrub. Cover berries with vinegar and soak over night. Drain off or squeeze out the juice, to every pint of which add one pound of sugar. Let it simmer about fifteen minutes; when cool, bottle, and when used as a drink put as much of it to a glass of water as is palatable to the invalid.

RASPBERRY ACID—*Mrs. Knox.*

Put twelve pounds of raspberries in an earthen jar; cover with two quarts of water with five ounces tartaric acid dissolved in water; let it remain forty-eight hours, then strain it and to each pint of juice add one and one-half pounds sugar; stir occasionally until dissolved; leave for a few days then bottle and cork lightly at first. If fermentation takes place leave the cork out a few days, then seal. The whole is made cold.

CURRANT ICE WATER.—*Mrs. Wheeler.*

Press the juice from ripe currauts, strain, add a pound of sugar to every pint of juice. The sugar may be dissolved either by stirring it in the juice in a saucepan over the fire, or by putting it in bottles, setting them over the fire in a saucepan of cold water, allowing them to become gradually heated to a boiling point. When cold they should be taken out, corked, sealed, and put in a cool, dry place. Mix with ice-water for a beverage. The juice of other acid fruits may be preserved in a like manner.

GINGER POP.—*Miss Carrie Perkins.*

Five and one-half gallons water, one-quarter of a pound of ginger-root bruised, one-half ounce tartaric acid, two and a half pounds white sugar, one gill yeast, one teaspoonful lemon oil, the whites of three eggs, well beaten.

Health and Beauty { Preserved and greatly enhanced by caring for the Teeth with Kalliodont.

Boil the root thirty minutes in one gallon water, strain off and put the oil in while the water is hot, then add the other materials. Make at night, and in the morning skim and bottle, keeping back the sediment.

EFFERVESCING FRUIT DRINKS.—*Mrs. Wheeler.*

Put strawberries, blackberries or raspberries into good vinegar, then strain off, adding fresh fruit until the flavor is agreeable. Bottle it and when about to use it, dissolve a small teaspoonful soda in a little water; when melted, nearly fill the tumbler with water, then add the fruit vinegar and drink immediately.

BEEF EXTRACT.

Soak finely chopped lean beef in an equal weight of cold water for an hour, then gradually raise to a boiling point. Simmer for fifteen minutes and strain.

BEEF TEA.

QUICKLY MADE.

Chop lean beef fine, and place it in a baking-pan, covering it with another pan, place it in a hot oven, and in fifteen minutes the juice will be ready to strain off.

J. Hutchison's Nurseries,

Corner 26th Street and Telegraph Avenue.

FLORAL AND  SEED DEPOT,

Corner 14th and Washington Streets,

Near the Post Office,   OAKLAND.

———o———

Has for sale the largest collection of Hardy Flowering and Ornamental Plants on the coast. Suitable for Parlor Windows, for the Flower Garden, for the Lawn, for Vases, for Rockeries, for Hanging Baskets, for Ribboning, for Hedges, for Arbors, for Shade Trees, for Shelter and for Timber.

Choice Flower Seed, Garden Seeds, Lawn Grass, End Clover Seed, etc.

Also, a splendid collection of Bulbs.

CUT FLOWERS and FLORAL DECORATIONS a specialty.

Good Gardeners recommended.

JAMES HUTCHISON,

Corner Fourteenth and Washington Streets,   OAKLAND.

MISCELLANEOUS.

JAPANESE CLEANING CREAM.

Take three ounces of white castile soap; shave it fine; put in it a quart of water and boil until dissolved, then add three quarts of water. When cool, add three ounces of ammonia, three of ether, three of alcohol, two of glycerine. Put all together and it is ready for use. Excellent for cleaning clothes, spots from carpets, etc., etc.

To wash flannels, make a suds of borax-soap and rinse in warm suds.

To renovate carpets or upholstered furniture, first beat out the dust, have ready a strong solution of Spanish bark, prepared by covering two pounds of bark with two gallons of cold water; let it steep all day slowly; when ready to use add more water, (use cold). Then scrub your carpets with this as you would a floor, using a small scrubbing brush; rub afterward with a dry linen cloth; proceed in the same way with furniture. This restores colors, removes grease and makes old things look new.

Calicos and Chambreys will not fade if before the first washing they are soaked for an hour in a bucket of cold water containing one tablespoonful of sugar of lead.

CELERY-SALT.

Save the root of the celery plant; dry and grate it, mixing it with one-third as much salt. Keep in a bottle well corked. It is delicious for soups, oysters, gravies, and hashes.

To prevent onion and cabbage odors—When cooking these vegetables or fish, set a tincup of vinegar on the stove and let it boil.

Salt will curdle new milk. Hence in preparing dishes from the latter, add salt after it is taken from the fire.

Lemons will keep better and fresher in water than any other way. After six weeks the peel will be fresh as the day they were put in.

When your kerosene lamps give a bad light, and smoke, or smell, boil the burners half an hour with a tablespoonful of soda in the water.

Swiss Confectionery, { **Ladies' and Gentlemen's Ice Cream and Coffee Saloon, 416 Twelfth Street. Wm. J. F. Laage, Prop.**

Ladies may avoid the injurious results occasioned by running sewing machines if, while sewing they sit upon a chair somewhat higher than is generally used at the machine.

Sufferers from asthma will find great relief and oftentimes a *permanent cure* in the prescription which J. H. Widber advertises in this book. We have used it and know its merits.

If you are troubled with ants, ask your druggist for a strong solution of corrosive sublimate; wipe your shelves with it and they will disappear. This is unfailing.

Glass bottles can be cut off below the neck and used for jelly glasses. Tie a cord around the bottle, wet with turpentine or coal oil and set fire to it. Try it.

To stop a creaking door, rub the hinges with hard soap.

Coal oil will soften boots and shoes that have been hardened by water.

To keep ice-water. Make a cover of two thicknesses of brown paper, with cotton batting quilted between, large enough to drop over and completely envelop the pitcher. This prevents the hot air from coming in contact with the pitcher. The ice will last a long time.

BRAN CAKE FOR DIABETES.—*Mrs. Mary Harmon.*

Take one quart of wheat bran; boil it in two successive waters for fifteen minutes, each time straining it through a sieve; then wash it well with cold water on the sieve until the water runs off perfectly clear; squeeze the bran in a cloth as dry as you can, then spread it thinly on a dish and place it in a slow oven; if put in at night, let it remain until morning, when, if perfectly dry and crisp, it will be fit for grinding. The bran thus prepared must be ground in a fine mill and sifted through a wire sieve of such fineness as to require a brush to pass it through. That which remains in the sieve must be ground again, until it becomes quite soft and fine. Take of this bran three ounces, some use four, and other ingredients as follows: Three new laid eggs, two ounces of butter, and one-half pint of milk; mix the eggs with a little of the milk, warm the butter with the other portion, then stir the whole together, adding a little nutmeg, or ginger, or any other kind of spice; bake in small tin pans, which must be well buttered, in a quick oven for about half an hour. The cakes when baked should be a little thicker than a captain's biscuit. To be eaten with butter or a curd of any of the soft cheeses.

CAMPHOR ICE.

One-half ounce gum camphor with alcohol enough to dissolve it, one-half ounce white wax, one-half ounce vassaline jelly. Put all together in a tin cup; heat enough to melt thoroughly.

NOTE.—The following is a table of measures and weights which will be found useful in connection with the recipes:

One quart of flour,............................one pound
Two coffee cups of butter........................ "
One generous pint of liquid...................... "
Two cupfuls of granulated sugar.................. "
Two heaping cupfuls of powdered sugar............ "
One pint finely-chopped meat, packed solidly..... "
The cup used is the common kitchen cup, holding half a pint.

RECIPE FOR HOUSEKEEPING.

Take one part self-control, one part discipline, five parts patience, and sweeten all with charity. Keep constantly on hand, and the domestic wheels will run smoothly.

Lovejoy's Patent Kitchen Cabinet is a marvel of mechanical skill and utility. No housekeeper should be without one. Chr. Schreiber, 1064 and 1066 Broadway, Oakland, is the agent for this Coast.

TO OUR READERS.

WE would call the attention of our patrons to the advertisements that appear on these pages. We have solicited from firms tried and trusted in their several lines, and they have been given us generously. Let us show our appreciation by giving them, in return, our patronage.

S. FRANCIS,
MERCHANT TAILOR,
BENITZ BLOCK,
1006 BROADWAY, { THREE DOORS FROM TENTH STREET, } **OAKLAND.**

---o---

☞ Fine Selection of Foreign and Domestic Cloths, Beavers and Cassimeres, made in the latest styles.

MOUNT & BUTEAU,
POULTRY, GAME,
Fruit and Produce,
STALLS 1, 3 AND 5 CITY MARKET,
415, 417 and 419 Twelfth Street, Oakland.

The National Gold Medal.

OAKLAND,   *CALIFORNIA.*

Horace Davis' Flour at Fish & Co's, Eighth and Market.

WM. B. HARDY,

Bookseller and Stationer,

961 BROADWAY, OAKLAND.

KAHN & SONS,
REMOVED

From Broadway and Twelfth Streets

TO

1003 BROADWAY, near Tenth Street,

FORMERLY KNOWN AS RED HOUSE.

A. HOENISCH,
Practical Upholsterer,

867 WASHINGTON STREET, OAKLAND.

☛ Furniture and Bedding made to order and repaired.   Work Guaranteed. Charges moderate.

H. J. McAVOY,
(Successor to GEO. S. HENRY,)

DEALER IN

Wood and Coal,

CHARCOAL AND COKE,

Southeast Corner 10th and Washington Sts.

OAKLAND, CAL.

W. W. MONTAGUE & CO.

IMPORTERS OF AND DEALERS IN

STOVES, RANGES

— AND —

House Furnishing Goods.

PLUMBING, ROOFING & GAS FITTING.

PACKER'S ICE CREAM FREEZERS—Freeze in 15 Minutes.

1152 BROADWAY,

Northeast Corner Thirteenth Street,   OAKLAND.

Pure Glycerine Toilet Soap

MADE BY

B. T. LEAKE,

AND SOLD ONLY BY HIM AT

No. 1313 West Street, Oakland, Cal.

R. E. BELL,

DRUGGIST,

Junction Telegraph Avenue and Broadway,

OAKLAND, CAL.

Pure, Fresh, Sweet Drugs.   *Full Line of Druggists' Sundries.*

☞ Prescriptions carefully compounded, Day and Night.

If you want { Good Stamping for Embroidery, go to Miss J. S. Naismith's, 1161 Broadway.

M. DE LA MONTANYA,

DEALER IN

Ranges, Stoves & Tinware,

465 ELEVENTH STREET,

Between Broadway and Washington,   OAKLAND, CAL.

All kinds of Tin, Copper, Zinc and Sheet-Iron Work Made to Order.

Metal Roofing and Plumbing in all their Branches.

☞ Repairing done at Short Notice, and at the Lowest Rates. ☜

THE WONDER

FLOWER AND FEATHER STORE,

1024 MARKET STREET, SAN FRANCISCO.

Will undersell any House in the City.

The Name above and below the Window.

New Goods

JUST RECEIVED
AT WAY DOWN PRICES.

Heavy Ottoman Silk, $1.
New Shades Summer Silks, 75c.
Elegant Brocaded Silk, $1 25.
Heavy Gros Grain Dress Silk, $1 75.
Extra Quality Dress Silk, $2 50.
28 inches wide Silk Velvet, $2 50.
48 inches All-Wool Dress Goods, new shades, 50c.
Extra Quality 44 inches, Colored and Black Cashmere, 75c.

100 Pieces Silk and-Wool Plaids, 20c.
150 Pieces Double Width English Cashmere, 25c.
200 Pieces Fine Seersucker, 12½c.
100 Pieces Good Washing Gingham, 8c.
50 Cases Straw Hats at Half Price.
150 Pieces Lace Worked Pique, 10c
Special Bargains in Laces, Corsets and Lisle Gloves.

A Full Line of **BOOTS** and **SHOES** at Very Low Prices.

A. LIPPMANN & CO.

903 and 905 Broadway, two doors above Eighth Street, **Oakland**.

Dr. Merriman's { Fragrant Kalliodont, Beautifies, Preserves the Teeth, and Charms all who use it.

BLAKE HOUSE.

This well known and popular House,

1059 WASHINGTON STREET,

Within four blocks of Broadway Station, is now under the management of

MRS. M. H. BLAKE.

the founder. It is centrally located and has large and commodious rooms, en suite or single, and extensive grounds with excellent table. *Terms Reasonable.*

ARTISTS' MATERIALS
—AND—
PICTURE FRAMES,

Whittier, Fuller & Co.

412 and 414 Twelfth Street, Oakland, Cal.

BURTCHAELL & CROWLEY,

Plumbers, Gas and Steam Fitters,

1208 BROADWAY,

Opposite Post Office,   OAKLAND, CAL.

—o—

Pump repairing and general jobbing.   Sanitary Plumbing a specialty.
All Work Warranted.

WM. T. HAMILTON,
UNDERTAKER
— AND —
CORONER OF ALAMEDA COUNTY,

Has removed to his New Building,

No. 466 THIRTEENTH STREET,

Between Broadway and Washington,   OAKLAND.

- Everything requisite for Funerals.
- Orders attended to day or night, or by Telephone.

Use Kelsey & Flint's Flavoring Extracts.

LIFE
INSURANCE COMPANY.

Assets,   -   - $51,600,000

Surplus, (by New York standard) $7,800,000

With *Thirty-Seven Years' Experience,* this stands *in the front rank,* in everything that makes up a desirable company, in which to insure one's life.

JAMES B. ROBERTS,

GENERAL AGENT,

315 California Street,

SAN FRANCISCO.

Swiss Confectionery, { Ladies' and Gentlemen's Ice Cream and Coffee Saloon, 416 Twelfth Street. Wm. J. F Laage, Prop.

BENNISON, LIEBMANN & CO.

IMPORTERS AND DEALERS IN

DRY GOODS, FANCY GOODS,

Trimmings, Embroideries, Hosiery, Gloves, Etc., Etc.

1157 and 1159 Broadway,

Between Thirteenth and Fourteenth Streets,   OAKLAND, CAL.

JAMES DALZIEL,

Pioneer Stove Store,

1465 SAN PABLO AVENUE,

Opposite Nineteenth Street,   OAKLAND, CAL.

JOHN M. ADAMS,

(SUCCESSOR TO H. C. PRATT,)

DEALER IN

WOOD AND COAL,

HAY, GRAIN AND FEED,

Cor. Telegraph Ave. and 26th St. (Bay Place) Oakland, Cal.

TELEPHONE FROM PORTER BROS.

BECKER'S MARKET,

817 Broadway,

Between Fifth and Sixth Streets,   OAKLAND.

———o———

FRED. BECKER, - - - - Proprietor.

E. A. Brown, { Wholesale and Retail Dealer in Wood and Coal, 410 and 412 Ninth Street.

GO TO

J. H. WIDBER'S

and ask for

Pres. 178,749.

IT IS PREPARED IN LIQUID FORM, AND IS AN

UNFAILING CURE FOR ASTHMA.

TO PROMOTE AN APPETITE FOR THE GOOD THINGS contained in this book,

TAKE A RIDE TO
Piedmont Springs

In one of those fine open cars that leave Seventh and Washington streets, in pleasant weather, upon the arrival of trains from San Francisco, and leave the Post Office four minutes later.

O. & P. R. R. CO.

A. KLINE,
IMPORTER OF

FANCY GOODS, LADIES' UNDERWEAR,

Gloves, Hosiery, Buttons, Fringes,

Gimp, Ribbons, Zephyrs, Worsteds,

CANVASSES, BEADS, TRIMMINGS, ETC.

1111 BROADWAY,

Between Twelfth and Thirteenth Streets, **OAKLAND.**

Wm. K. Rowell, } Notary Public and Conveyancer, 458 Ninth Street, residence 410 Thirteenth St., First House East of Broadway, Oakland.

E. W. LUECKE.   F. M. REED.

Miss F. M. Reed & Co.

IMPORTERS OF

Fine French Millinery,

1161 BROADWAY, OAKLAND.

FOR PURE

Drugs, Toilet Articles and Perfumery,

GO TO

Dr. Fearn's Pharmacy,

Corner Tenth and Washington Streets,   Oakland.

—o—

Prescriptions carefully compounded. Everything warranted of FIRST QUALITY. Try the LONDON POMADE and HAIR TONIC. The BEST Preparation for the Hair.

J. HOMER FRITCH,

IMPORTER AND DEALER IN

WOOD AND COAL,

ETC., ETC.

Office, 413 Eleventh Street, Oakland.

It's Hope that keeps us up,
It's Hope that keeps our memories green,
It's Hope that makes our lives sublime,
It's LANZ BROS. SOAP that keeps us clean.

ASK YOUR GROCER FOR IT.

Factory and Salesroom,

911-913 Third Street, near Market,   **Oakland.**

The wife and daughter of a prominent citizen assures us they feel that they cannot do without Kalliodont.

TRADE MARK
ROYAL SEMI. PORCELAIN
JOHN MADDOCK & SONS
ENGLAND

ROYAL
SEMI-PORCELAIN
DINNER
AND
TEA WARE,

NEW "CHAIN PATTERN."

———o———

This ware is a perfect *fac simile* of French China, equal in color and finish, and more durable. Buyers will notice that each article bears the above Trade Mark, as there are many imitations in the market.

FOR SALE IN SETS OR SINGLE PIECES.

O. LAWTON & CO.

SOLE AGENTS,

16 Post Street,   San Francisco.

Every lady { Should advise her husband to carry an accident policy in The Travelers.

Wakefield Rattan Chairs.

For comfort and durability unexcelled by any other style.

We have now in stock the very finest assortment ever offered on this coast.

The accompanying *cut* represents our large Franklin Rocker No. 475 at $12.00.

We call particular attention to our

KURRACHEE RUGS,

New, chaste and elegant designs; in beautiful combinations of colors. We offer a better Rug for less money than any other house in San Francisco.

WAKEFIELD RATTAN CO.
644 Market Street,
SAN FRANCISCO

FRANK ORRA,
FRUIT AND VEGETABLE VENDER

Garden, 2025 East 14th Street,
EAST OAKLAND, CAL.

Pure Cream Tartar at Kelsey & Flint's.

A GOOD PLACE FOR LADIES TO GO FOR

OYSTERS,

California Market, Stalls 57, 58 and 59,

SOLOMON TESMORE.

Be Sure to go to the Right Number.

Contra Costa Packing Co.

RICE & WHITE, Proprietors.

Wholesale and Retail Dealers in First-Class Meats.

Smoked Beef, Pork, Bacon and Tongues always on hand.   Sausages a specialty.

Stalls 2, 4 and 6 City Market, Oakland.

☞ Entrance on Twelfth Street.

Coal Oil Stoves FOR FAMILY COOKING. ALSO, MANY OTHER HOUSEHOLD UTENSILS, SUCH AS—

Apple Parers,	Fry Pans,	Mouse Traps,	Spoons, Wood and Basting,
Broilers,	Fly Traps,	Meat Roasters,	Steam Cooker,
Button-Hole Scissors,	Fruit Canning Ladles,	Nut Crackers,	Tea Pot Stands,
Bread Toasters,	Gas Stoves,	Nutmeg Graters,	Tea Strainers,
Clothes Wringers,	Gasoline Stoves,	Oil Stoves,	Tracing Wheels,
Can Openers,	Graters,	Plaiters,	Tidy Pins,
Clothes Horses,	Irons, Mrs. Potts,	Plate Lifters,	Towel Racks,
Corn Poppers,	Jelly Pressers,	Peach Parers,	Telephones,
Coffee Roasters,	Knife Sharpeners,	Pocket Stoves,	Vegetable Boilers,
Corkscrews,	Laundry Lists,	Potato Fryers,	Wick Trimmers,
Cherry Stoners,	Lamp Chim. Cleaners,	Polish for Silverware,	Window Cleaners,
Egg Beaters,	Lanterns,	Potato Mashers,	Water Filters,
Fire Shovels,	Lemon Squeezers,	Rat Traps,	Washing Machines.
Flour Sifters,	Lawn Fountains,	Stovepipe Shelves,	
Fluting Machines,	Lap Boards, Folding,	Skates, Roller, &c.	

Wiester & Co., MANUFACTURERS AND DEALERS IN USEFUL INVENTIONS, 17 New Montgomery St., San Francisco.

FURNISS' RESTAURANT.

YOU CAN GET

A First-Class Meal

Any time between 6 A. M. and 9 P. M. for

25 CENTS

AT FURNISS' RESTAURANT,

Cor. 8th and Washington Sts., Oakland.

Coffee's Old Auction House, corner Broadway and Eighth Street.

LADIES' LUNCH ROOM,

SWAIN'S,

213 SUTTER STREET,

SAN FRANCISCO.

{ Ladies' Hair Dressing. } *Wholesale and Retail.* { Practical Wig Making. }

GOLDSTEIN & COHN,

IMPORTERS OF

HUMAN HAIR,

And Manufacturers of SWITCHES, CURLS, CHIGNONS, &c.

822 MARKET STREET,

PHELAN'S BUILDING,   SAN FRANCISCO.

Theatricals and Masquerade Wigs to let. { COMBINGS MADE UP IN ANY STYLE. COUNTRY ORDERS promptly attended to. } Ladies' and Children's Hair Cutting.

WILLIAM NELLE,

First Class Meat Market,

371 TWELFTH STREET, CENTRAL AVENUE,

Oakland, Cal.

SLAVEN'S
California Fruit Salt.

BETTER THAN GOLD  **And as Pleasant as LEMONADE.**

FOR SALE BY ALL DRUGGISTS.

JOHN A. McKINNON.   DUDLEY C. BROWN.

BROWN & McKINNON,
MERCHANT TAILORS,
1020 Broadway,

Between 10th and 11th Streets,   OAKLAND, CAL

RUBBER GOODS.
Our Specialty, the "MALTESE CROSS" Brand.
Garden Hose, Rubber Gloves,
GOSSAMER CIRCULARS, HOT WATER BAGS, FLOWER SPRINKLERS,

Old Wringer-Rollers re-covered and made good as new.

THE GUTTA PERCHA AND RUBBER MANUFACTURING CO.
JOHN W. TAYLOR, Manager.

Corner First and Market Streets,   San Francisco.

A. J. MASON,
DEALER IN
Foreign and Domestic Coals,
WOOD, COKE AND CHARCOAL.
Corner Market and Eighth Streets,
OAKLAND, CAL.

R. W. MERRICK,
Baker and Confectioner,
960 Washington Street, between 9th and 10th,
OAKLAND.

Weddings and Parties supplied on shortest notice. Boston Brown Bread and Baked Beans delivered hot to Customers every Sunday Morning. Delicious ICE CREAM made to order.

CHAS. W. BONNEY.   FRANK J. BONNEY

CHAS. W. BONNEY & CO,
Dealers in all kinds of
WOOD, COAL,
COKE AND CHARCOAL.
Office and Yard—462 Thirteenth Street,

Between Broadway and Washington,   OAKLAND, CAL.

JAS. M. TORREY.   W. W. WHITMAN.   J. T. GARDINER

TORREY, WHITMAN & GARDINER,
GROCERS,
461 and 463 Eleventh St., near Broadway,
OAKLAND, CAL.

TAFT & PENNOYER,

IMPORTERS OF

STAPLE & FANCY DRY GOODS,

1163 AND 1165 BROADWAY,

OAKLAND, CAL.

Sole Agents for { Butterick Patterns and Publications.
Catalogues Sent on Application.
John A. Cutter & Co.'s Silks.

PHILADELPHIA
CHEMICAL STEAM DYEING & CLEANING WORKS,

CHAS. REUTER, Proprietor.

Office and Works—833, 835 and 837 Washington Street,

Between Sixth and Seventh,   OAKLAND, CAL.

Ladies' Shawls and Dresses finished like new, with punctuality.
Gentlemen's Clothing cleaned, dyed and repaired.

WILL H. BURRALL,
NOTARY PUBLIC,
CONVEYANCER,

REAL ESTATE AND LOAN AGENT.

Office---No. 1106 Broadway,

First Door North of Twelfth Street,   OAKLAND, CAL.

B. SCHONWASSER & CO.

IMPORTERS AND MANUFACTURERS OF

Ladies', Children's and Infants' Wear,

134 Post Street, Corner Dupont,

SAN FRANCISCO,

INFANTS WARDROBES A SPRCIALTY.

{ B. SCHONWASSER,
{ MAX DAVIS.

DECKER PIANOS

Have shown themselves to be so far superior to all others in excellence of *Workmanship*, *Elasticity of Touch*, *Beauty of Tone*, and great *Durability*, that they are now earnestly sought for by all persons desiring

THE VERY BEST PIANO.

CAUTION.—All genuine Decker Pianos have the following name (precisely here shown) on the Pianos above the keys:

| Prices Low. | Decker Brothers, New York. | Easy Terms. |

☛Send for Illustrated Catalogue.

KOHLER & CHASE, San Francisco,
Wholesale and Retail Agents for Pacific States.

BRANCH STORE, Corner Ninth and Washington Sts., Oakland, Cal.

M. S. SMITH & CO.

MANUFACTURERS OF

FRAMES

DEALERS IN ARTISTS' MATERIALS,

Mouldings, Engravings, Chromos, School Books, Stationery and Toys.

1154 Broadway,   **Oakland, Cal.**

CHICAGO MARKET,

SMEDER & DONALDSON,

Wholesale and Retail Dealers in

Beef, Veal, Mutton, Lamb, Pork, Hams,

BACON, LARD AND SAUSAGE.

Vegetables, Poultry and Game in season. Goods promptly delivered free.

964 Broadway, between 9th and 10th Streets,   **Oakland.**

☞ Liberal Discount allowed to Hotels, Boarding Houses and Vessels.

G. ABRAHAMSON,

IMPORTER OF

FANCY GOODS, TRIMMINGS, ETC.

110 KEARNY STREET,

Between Post and Sutter,   *San Francisco.*

1117 Broadway, Bet. 12th and 13th Streets, Oakland.

C. F. EDWARDS. F. J. EDWARDS.

EDWARDS BROS.

(Formerly of Sutter Street Market, San Francisco,)

WHOLESALE AND RETAIL DEALERS IN

Fresh, Smoked and Salt Fish,

California and Eastern Oysters, Clams, Crabs, Shrimps, &c.

468 Eleventh Street,

Between Broadway and Washington, OAKLAND.

Restaurants, Families, Hotels and Shipping supplied at the shortest notice and on the most reasonable terms. Orders delivered free of charge to any part of the City.

M. CALISHER,

Bookseller and Stationer,

1119 BROADWAY,

Cor. Thirteenth Street, OAKLAND.

Ladies' Stationery a Specialty.

T. S. CLARK. L. C. CLARK.

TRUMAN S. CLARK & CO.

MANUFACTURERS OF

WOVEN WIRE MATTRESSES

AND GAS PIPE IRON BEDSTEADS

Of every Style and Quality.

OFFICE AND MANUFACTORY, **21 New Montgomery Street,** Under Grand Hotel, SAN FRANCISCO.

VAN STAN'S STRATENA.

BEST CEMENT IN THE WORLD!

MENDS EVERYTHING!

FOR SALE BY ALL DRUGGISTS.

SADLER & CO., San Francisco, Sole Agents.

BROWN'S
Livery, Sale AND Boarding Stable,

518 Thirteenth Street, Oakland, Cal.

JAS. A. BROWN & CO., - - *Proprietors.*

This Stable being new, centrally located, and supplied with all the latest improvements, affords convenience to the general public.

BUGGIES
AND
CARRIAGES

With good, gentle Horses on reasonable terms.

Special Attention paid to Boarding and Transient Horses.

JAMES LENTELL,
MANUFACTURER AND DEALER IN
Harness, Saddles, Whips,
HORSE-CLOTHING,
Blankets and Lap Robes,
CAMRON BLOCK,
469 and 471 Fourteenth Street,
Between Post Office and City Hall, Oakland.

A fine line of Single and Double Harness always on hand and for sale at low prices. No necessity to go to San Francisco to buy Harness, or for anything that is kept in a well-regulated Harness Shop.

Goods guaranteed as represented. Repairing neatly and promptly executed. PLEASE CALL AND EXAMINE MY STOCK.

L. BURBANK,

961 Washington Street, Oakland,

Keeps constantly on hand a large assortment of

Ladies', Misses' & Children's Shoes.

ALSO, MEN'S, BOYS' AND YOUTHS'.

Custom Work and Repairing a specialty.

THOMSON BROTHERS, - - - - Proprietors.

THOMSON'S BAKERY,

Fresh Milk, French and American Bread,

Boston Brown Bread and Pork and Beans every Sunday Morning.

No. 1218 BROADWAY,

Opposite Post Office,   OAKLAND, CAL

☞ All kinds of Fancy and Ornamental Cakes for Weddings and Parties.

A. ROBINSON,

STEAM CARPET BEATING ESTABLISHMENT

519 Second Street, Oakland, Cal.

—o—

CARPETS taken up, cleaned and delivered the same day.
CARPETS cut, sewed and laid in first class style.
All orders by mail promptly attended to.

THE LATEST STYLES IN

SPRING GOODS

Arriving DAILY at the

New York Dry and Fancy Goods House,

E. ABRAHAMS,

913 Broadway, bet. 8th and 9th,   Oakland.

Sign of the GOLDEN HORSE SHOE.

Established A. D. 1821.

PACIFIC DEPARTMENT

ASSURANCE COMPANY

OF LONDON.

o

Paid-up Capital, - - $5,000,000 00
Total Fire Funds, - - $7,652,313 16

o

WM. J. LANDERS, General Agent, San Francisco.
B. C. HAWES, City Agent, 314 California Street.

Use Yale Locks for Safety

FRONT DOOR LOCKS, CUPBOARD LOCKS, SMALL BRONZE PADLOCKS, ETC., ETC.

FOR SALE BY THE

HARDWARE TRADE,

—AND—

RICHARDS & SNOW,

406 and 408 Market Street, San Francisco.

THE

OAKLAND TRIBUNE

Has the largest circulation and is the most influential journal published on the Pacific Coast outside of San Francisco.

THE

WEEKLY TRIBUNE

Is an epitome of the week's news, with special articles interesting to the agriculturist, and is a great favorite with those residing in the country.

The TRIBUNE PUBLISHING COMPANY has a complete

Job Office and Book Bindery,

and can execute anything in those branches in a first-class manner, at reasonable rates.

J. P. O'TOOLE & CO.

——IMPORTERS OF——

DRY GOODS,

953 WASHINGTON STREET,

OAKLAND.

D. RYAN,

DRUGGIST AND APOTHECARY,

1170 BROADWAY,

Near Fourteenth Street,   OAKLAND, CAL.

Ladies' Dress Hats,
    Misses' School and Dress Hats,
        Chip, Leghorn,
            Milan, Fancy Straws,

IN ALL SHAPES AND COLORS CHEAPEST AT

JONES',

Headquarters for Feathers.   **907 Broadway, Oakland.**

FRENCH LAUNDRY,

1169 Washington Street,

Near 14th Street,   Oakland.

Fine Washing Laces and Curtains done up like new.
Lace Curtains a specialty.

HALLS SAFE AND LOCK CO.

211 and 213 California Street, San Francisco.

MANUFACTURERS OF

HALLS' STANDARD FIRE AND BURGLAR PROOF SAFES,

Vaults, Time Locks, Etc.

Second hand SAFES bought, sold, exchanged and repaired.   SAFES sold on easy Installments.

C. B. PARCELLS,   -   -   -   **Manager.**

Too Late for Classification.

A chapter of Cooking Recipes and things worth knowing, received too late for classification.

COFFEE.—*Mrs. James B. Roberts.*

Select good coffee, according to one's taste; "Old Government Java," if it can be procured. Roast to a chestnut brown, so that it will grind readily; roast evenly, and discard all grains burned black. When almost cold (before grinding) stir the white of one egg into a pound of coffee, thoroughly.

Keep it from exposure to the air, thus preserving the aroma as much as possible. Grind the coffee moderately fine; put a teacupful in the pot, which must be hot; pour on a quart of boiling water, and let it stand, say ten minutes, before using. Clarify it by pouring in a few tablespoonsful of cold water. It can be adapted to one's taste by adding sugar, cream, milk, or hot water. It must not be boiled a moment; and pots in which coffee has been boiled must not be used without a thorough purification by scalding water.

Such coffee, a life insurance policy in the "Connecticut Mutual Life Insurance Company," and a conscience "void of offense toward God and man," will conduce greatly to the peace, comfort and happiness of any family.

HOW TO CARVE AT TABLE.

First, as to tools, let the knife be of the keenest and the fork of the sharpest, and keep them in excellent condition at all times, otherwise the most competent carver cannot avoid mangling fish, flesh and fowl. Before setting the carver to work, it may be well to advise as to what may be called carver's etiquette. When carving do not stand up, or sit with arms akimbo, or bow the back. All the necessary strength can be brought to bear while seated by inclining the body sufficiently forward. During all the pauses in the carving, the knife and fork should be placed in the knife rest, and never thrust under what is being carved. Nor should the knife and fork be held in one hand while adding the gravy with the spoon in the other. Do not tilt the

---

MISS E. S. BUELL, { Decorative Art Rooms. Fancy Work of all Kinds.
1118 Washington Street, Oakland.

dish while serving the gravy, or the tablecloth may be soiled or the roast capsized. Should there be no gravy well, a tiny crust of bread may be placed under one end of the dish to cant it a little. Serve horseradish with the fork. Up to the moment of using, the gravy spoon should be in a vessel of hot water placed at the right hand of the dish. Hot plates are essential to the perfect condition of roast meat; even a second hot plate for a second helping. It is scarcely necessary to caution the carver not to forget to ask what the preference is before carving.

When carving fish, if salmon, avoid breaking the flakes by dividing crosswise; carry the knife down to the bone lengthwise of the fish, and remove a slice of either the thick or thin part, as preferred. Mackerel are split at the tail, and the upper half raised from the bone at that part; the bone is removed and the lower half served either entire or divided into sections. This applies to most other small fish.

In carving a turkey or chicken, roasted or boiled, place it with the neck toward you; take off the leg at the first joint and then the thigh, or take off the whole leg and then joint it. Remove the wing close to the joint, leaving the breast intact. Then commence from the wing joint, cutting straight into the bone and somewhat diagonally up to the front of the breast-bone. Remove the side bones by placing the fork firmly into the breast-bone and cutting with the knife from the tail end.

With a goose or duck, after the joints are removed, as already described, draw the knife straight across the breast-bone the entire length of the meat and directly to the bone, serving outwardly and with parts of the meat from the thigh.

SPINACH SOUP. *Mrs. Chickering.*

Boil one quart spinach. Chop fine and pass through a sieve or colander. Put this into one qnart boiling milk thickened with one *scant* tablespoonful of corn starch mixed in a little cold milk. Put into the soup pot two ounces butter, season with salt, pepper, and a dash of nutmeg. Turn out into a hot tureen.

TOMATO SOUP WITHOUT MEAT.—*Mrs Chas. Ames.*

Put a lump of butter about the size of a walnut into the pot, slice some three or four onions very fine, fry until brown, stirring frequently, not to burn or scorch in the least, then turn in your tomatoes

---

Swiss Confectionery. { **Ladies' and Gentlemen's Ice Cream and Coffee Saloon,** 416 Twelfth Street. Wm. J. F Laage, Prop.

and thin to the right consistency by putting in hot water; just before bringing to the table thicken a little cream with flour and stir in, and let come to a boil, then season with red pepper, and salt, and bring on smoking hot.

MAYONNAISE FOR SALADS, FISH, ETC.—*Mrs. Marwedel.*

Into the yolks of two raw eggs beat *slowly* about a teacupful of sweet oil, using a wire spoon. If it thickens too rapidly add a little of the white to thin it, before using all of the oil. Add salt, cayenne pepper and lime-juice to suit the taste. The whites beaten to a stiff froth may also be added the last thing.

MOCK GINGER PRESERVES.

Cut into strips the thick rind of a watermelon, trim off the green and cut out the inside until the rind is firm; cover with water, into which throw enough soda to make the water taste of it; let stand from twelve to twenty-four hours; take out, boil in clear water until a straw will go easily through; drain; put into syrup made of good brown sugar, very strongly flavored with pounded ginger; let boil slowly until the syrup penetrates the rind. This is almost as good as ginger preserve. A beautiful preserve may be made by cutting the rind into fancy shapes, and substituting white sugar and lemons cut in thin rounds for the ginger and brown sugar. Soda makes the rind more brittle than alum or lime.

To keep jellies from moulding, pulverize loaf sugar and cover the surface of the jelly to the depth of quarter of an inch; this will prevent mould even though the jellies are kept for years.

CURRANT JELLY.—*Mrs. Knox.*

Pick over (but not stem) the currants and put over the fire. Let them boil until the fruit is broken to pieces; strain through a bag. To each pint or bowl of juice allow same quantity of sugar. Set the juice on alone to boil, and while it is warming put the sugar into shallow pie dishes or pans that will fit in your ovens. Boil the juice hard for just *three* minutes *after* it begins to boil, skimming off the scum as it rises. By this time the sugar should be as hot as you can bear your hand in it. Throw the sugar into the boiling juice, stirring rapidly all the while; skim and boil *just two* minutes, and

---

Every lady { Should advise her husband to carry an accident policy in The Travelers.

remove at once from the fire. Roll your glasses or cups in hot water and fill with the scalding liquid.

SPICED CURRANTS.—*Mrs. Noah Kelsey.*

To six pounds of fresh ripe currants take four pounds brown sugar, one pint vinegar, one tablespoonful cinnamon, one tablespoonful of cloves, one tablespoonful allspice (spices ground). Let them all boil together three hours, or until they look well done.

COFFEE JELLY.—*Mrs. I. W. Knox.*

One pint coffee, three sheets gelatine, one and one-half tablespoonfuls sugar.

LEMON JELLY.—*Mrs. I. W. Knox.*

One pint water, two cups sugar, five sheets gelatine lemon to taste. The above jellies are very nice for dessert, together or singly, served with cream.

ICE CREAM, GOOD.—*Mrs. Wheeler.*

One quart of milk; when boiling, add five beaten eggs, one cup of sugar; cook ten minutes. Flavor with Merten, Moffitt & Co's extract of vanilla or lemon, and freeze rapidly. The success of this depends in a great degree upon constant and rapid turning of the freezer.

SELF-FREEZING ICE CREAM.—*Mrs. W. T. Kelsey.*

One quart rich milk, eight eggs, whites and yolks beaten separately and very light, four cups sugar (powdered) three pints rich, sweet cream, five teaspoonfuls vanilla or other seasoning, boiled in the custard and left in until cold. Heat the *milk* almost to boiling, beat the yolks light, add the sugar and stir up well. Pour the hot milk to this little by little, beating all the while; put in the frothed whites, and return to the fire boiling in a pail or saucepan set within one of hot water. Stir the mixture steadily about fifteen minutes, or until it is thick as boiled custard. Pour into a bowl and set aside to cool. When quite cold beat in the cream. For the flavoring use Merten, Moffitt & Co's

---

Dr. Merriman's { **Fragrant Kalliodont Beautifies and Preserves the Teeth.**

extract of lemon or vanilla and strain through a hair or *fine* sieve into the freezer.

DIRECTIONS FOR FREEZING WITHOUT A PATENT FREEZER.

Use an old-fashioned upright freezer or a *close-fitting* covered pail; set in a deep pail, pack around it closely first a layer of pounded ice, then one of rock salt, *common salt will not do.* In this order fill the pail; but before covering the freezer lid, remove it carefully that none of the salt may get in, and, with a long wooden ladle or flat stick beat the custard as you would batter, for five minutes without stay or stint. Replace the lid, pack the ice and salt upon it, patting it down hard on top; cover all with several folds of blanket or carpet and leave it for an hour, then remove the cover off the freezer when you have wiped it carefully outside. Dislodge with ladle or long·carving knife the thick coating of frozen custard on sides and bottom of freezer. Beat again hard and long until the custard is a smooth, half-congealed paste, say fifteen minutes, spread the double blanket or carpet over the freezer after it has been repacked with ice and salt, turn off the brine, leave for three hours. If the water accumulates in such quantity as to buoy up the freezer, pour it off, fill up with ice and salt, but do not open the freezer. In two hours more you may take it from the ice, open it, wrap a towel wrung out in boiling water about the lower part and turn out a solid column of cream, firm, close-grained, and smooth as velvet to the tongue.

VELVET CREAM.

Two tablespoons of gelatine, dissolved in a half-tumbler of water; one pint of rich cream; four tablespoonfuls of sugar; flavor with vanilla extract or rose water. Put in moulds and set on the ice. This is a delicious dessert, and can be made in a few minutes. It may be served with or without cream.

Whipped coffee cream for one who likes the coffee flavor is perfectly delicious as a last morsel at a formal dinner or an afternoon lunch. Take two ounces of coffee beans and roast them; while fresh and still warm put them in one pint of rich cream, which you have sweetened liberally with sugar. Let this stand for an hour; then strain through a muslin cloth laid in a colander; dissolve a teaspoonful of gelatine in a little cold milk, and add to the cream;

Try Fish & Co's Block Butter, Eighth and Market.

then whip it to a firm froth. The gelatine may be dissolved in a little orange water, or lemon extract if you choose.

CRYSTALLIZED ORANGES.

Crystallized fruits form a prominent feature in all confectioners' windows just now, and beguile boys and girls into spending all their spare money for them. If they care to take the trouble they can prepare oranges, at home, which will take the place at half the expense of the costly fruit. Peel and quarter the oranges, make a syrup of one pound of sugar to one pint of water, let this boil until it is like candy around the edge of the dish, then dip the oranges in this and let them drain; keep them where it is warm, and the candied syrup will become crystallized. Try this; it is delicious.

SOUR MILK BISCUIT.

Sift one quart flour containing one teaspoonful soda and one of cream tartar through a fine sieve, then add a teaspoonful of salt, a tablespoonful of butter; mix with sour milk stiff enough to roll out. Let them stand ten or fifteen minutes before baking, then bake in a moderately quick oven.

CORN MEAL MUFFINS.

Stir two cupfuls of cream or milk with the yolks of three well-beaten eggs. Sift together one cup of flour, two cups of yellow Indian meal, two teaspoonfuls of baking powder, a teaspoonful of salt, one tablespoonful of yellow sugar. Stir in the milk and eggs. Beat well together. Add, lastly, the well-beaten whites. Pour on well-buttered muffin rings. Bake in a well-heated oven and serve as soon as baked.

GREEN CORN CAKES.

Grate green corn and mix with milk, adding flour enough to make a batter stiff enough to hold the corn together; add a teaspoonful of yeast powder to a pint of batter and fry as you would griddle cakes.

RICE CAKES.

Take a pint bowl of cold boiled rice, three eggs, a little salt, one pint of milk, and flour sufficient for quite a stiff batter; add a scant teaspoon of yeast powder to the flour before mixing the other ingredients; fry in cakes in butter or lard.

Get your Baking Powder of Kelsey & Flint.

STUFFING FOR A TURKEY

For a turkey weighing from eight to ten pounds, allow one loaf of stale baker's bread, one quart of oysters, one lemon, two roots of celery and one-quarter of a pound of butter. It is taken for granted that the turkey is thoroughly cleaned and wiped dry before putting the stuffing in. Crumble the bread till very fine ; season with pepper and salt. Drain the oysters, setting the liquor aside. Now take a very sharp knife and peel off the outer rind of the lemon, being careful not to have any of the bitter and tough white skin left on ; cut the peel in very small bits ; chop the white part of the celery very fine, adding the butter and the juice of the lemon ; mix the ingredients mentioned, stirring until thoroughly mixed ; then proceed to stuff body and crop. A turkey of the size spoken of requires at least two hours' baking, and it should be basted frequently ; the liquor of the oysters should be put in the pan when the pan is first set in the oven, and this is to be used in basting. The giblets and liver should be cooked in a basin on top of the stove, then chopped very fine and when the gravy is made add them to it.

STUFFED TOMATOES BAKED.—*Mrs. Sherman.*

Choose large, fair tomatoes. Remove enough of the skin from the top to scoop out one-half or three-fourths of the inside. Mix with this for the stuffing, bread or cracker crumbs, as much salt and pepper as is desired, and a bit of butter for each tomato. Fill the tomatoes with this preparation, heaping full, and bake until thoroughly done.

PICCALILLI.—*Mrs. Wells.*

One gallon green tomatoes cut fine ; salt them in layers, let them stand over night, then drain them well ; one tablespoon allspice, two of ground cloves, six green peppers, six onions, cut fine, one pint of white mustard, two teacups sugar ; put into a kettle, cover with vinegar and scald till tender.

IDEAL LEMON PIE.—*Mrs. Kelsey.*

Line some pie tins with puff paste, and bake so as to keep the filling from soaking. Take a firm lemon and grate the rind into a bowl and squeeze in the juice ; add to that one cup of white sugar

---

Swiss Confectionery, } Ladies' and Gentlemen's Ice Cream and Coffee Saloon, 416 Twelfth Street. Wm. J. F. Laage, Prop.

and the yolk of one egg stirred well together, then add one large cup cold water into which has been stirred a dessertspoonful of corn starch. Put into a saucepan and stir until it is a rich, clear straw-colored jelly. Put the filling into the crust and cover with a meringue made of the white and put it into the oven for an instant.

LEMON PIE.—*Mrs. S. H. Harmon.*

Juice of three lemons if juicy, if not, four or five; yolks of three eggs and one whole egg mixed together with one cup of sugar, and strain. Pour this custard into a plate lined with puff paste and bake. Meringue—Whites of three eggs beaten to a stiff froth; add two tablespoonfuls sugar. Put on top of custard when baked.

CUSTARD PUDDING.—*Mrs. Sherman.*

One quart milk, eight tablespoonfuls flour, eight eggs, beaten separately, and a little salt. Steam or bake three-fourths of an hour or until done.

SAUCE FOR THE SAME.

Two cups of fine sugar, one-half cup butter beaten to a cream, nutmeg to taste, and enough boiling milk added to make it the desired consistency.

BOILED INDIAN PUDDING

Three pints of milk, one pint of meal, five eggs; sweeten and flavor to taste. Boil in a cloth two or three hours; to be eaten with butter.

DELICATE CAKE.

One cup corn starch, one cup butter, one cup milk, two cups sugar, two cups flour, whites of seven eggs. Mix butter and sugar to a cream,; add two teaspoonfuls baking powder to the flour and corn starch, then add the flour, then the eggs; flavor to taste. Never fails to be good.

CHAMPAGNE CAKE. —*Mrs. M. P. Downing.*

One cup of sugar one-third cup butter, one-half cup milk, two-cups flour, one egg, one-half teaspoon soda, one cream tartar, nutmeg. This makes a good jelly cake—also a marble cake. Reserve

---

Pure Cream Tartar at Kelsey & Flint's.

one cup of the dough and stir in three tablespoons of grated chocolate. Drop this into the white part and give a little stir to marble it nicely.

THE BEST SANDWICHES.

To make wonderfully appetizing sandwiches proceed in this way: Take equal quantities of the breast of a cold boiled chicken and of cold boiled tongue. Chop them very fine; so fine, in fact, that you cannot distinguish the separate particles. Add a good, large half teaspoonful Merten, Moffitt & Co's. celery salt, a pinch of cayenne pepper, four tablespoonfuls of Mayonnaise dressing. This quantity of condiments will be enough to season the breast of one large chicken, and an equal quantity of tongue. When this is perfectly cold, spread some thin slices of bread with butter, and then with this mixture. Do not prepare them till you are about ready to serve them. If you wish to take sandwiches for a lunch when traveling, be careful not to make the dressing quite so moist as you would if they were to be eaten at home. The better way, if you do not object to the trouble, is to put the salad filling in a small glass jar and spread the sandwiches as you need them.

SILVERING SOLUTION.

We take pleasure in recommending Merten, Moffitt & Co's. Silvering solution as being the best of anything we have ever used to polish silver, washstand faucets, or any plated ware that has become tarnished or worn. Ask your druggist or grocer for it.

TO PRESERVE GREEN GOOSEBERRIES

Fill the jars with fresh berries, gathered while green, and fill up with cold water, seal the jars tightly and set in a cool place.

Every household has long felt the need of a furniture polish which conld be used without employing an expert to apply it. We have at last found what we desired in Merten, Moffiitt & Co's. Furniture Polish. Ons trial will convince you of its great superiority. Ask your grocer for it.

For Poison Oak.—Bathe freely with ammonia.

If troubled with indigestion, take one tablespoonful lime water in a goblet of milk at meals.

Keep an oyster shell in your tea kettle and it will prevent the formation of a crust on the inside of it, by attracting the stony particles to itself.

Cure for Consumption, at Fish & Co's, Eighth and Market.

To keep out moths, use pulverized alum; to drive away cockroaches, use Pulverized Borax; to rid your premises of rats and mice use "Rough on Rats." All of which you can purchase of H. Bowman, druggist, 951 Broadway, corner of Ninth.

BREAKFAST AT HOME.

"Well, madam," said the head of the house, who has apparently got out of bed on the wrong side, "what have you got for breakfast this morning? Boiled eggs, hey? Seems to me you never have anything but boiled eggs. Boiled Erebus! and what else, madam, may I ask?" "Mutton chops, my dear," says the wife, timidly. "Mutton chops!" echoes the husband, bursting into a peal of sardonic laughter. Mutton chops! I could have guessed it. By the living jingo, madam, if ever I eat another meal in this house"—— and jamming on his hat and slamming the door, the aggrieved man bounds down the stairs and betakes himself to the restaurant. "What'll you have, sir?" says the waiter, politely, handing him a bill of fare. "Oh!" says the guest, having glanced over it; "let me see! bring me two boiled egggs and a mutton chop."

A Toilet { Is incomplete without Dr. Merriman's Fragrant Kallio:ont.

IF YOU WOULD HAVE

ICE CREAM

Frozen rapidly and smoothly, and FREE FROM ICY LUMPS, use the

TRIPLE-MOTION

White Mountain Freezer.

☞ THE BEST IN THE WORLD! ☜

BECAUSE

It Freezes more Rapidly, uses Less Ice, requires Less Labor, and is More Durable than any other Freezer made.

For sale by all first-class dealers in House Furnishing Goods.

Holbrook, Merrill & Stetson,

Cor. Market and Beale Streets, San Francisco,

SOLE AGENTS FOR THE PACIFIC COAST.

Horace Davis' Flour at Fish & Co's, Eighth and Market.

NO BOBBINS.   NO SHUTTLE.   NO TENSION.

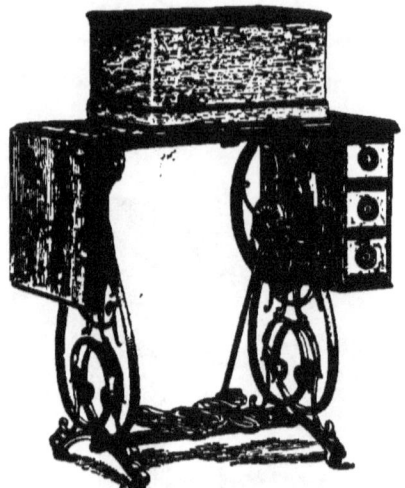

Lightest Running Sewing Machine in the World!

Noiseless.   Rapid.   Perfect.

THE "AUTOMATIC"

Made **FAMOUS** by its wonderful merit!

Ladies who have thoroughly investigated it pronounce it PERFECT.

Work that is difficult or impossible to do on **two thread tension machines,** is executed by the "AUTOMATIC" with marvelous ease and rapidity. The lady with sensitive nerves; the invalid, or the child can run it without injury to health—a claim that cannot be justly made for any other machine.

NOTE THE FOLLOWING.—We, the undersigned ladies of Oakland, California, take pleasure in testifying to the great superiority of the "AUTOMATIC" Sewing Machine over all others. We know from personal knowledge and experience of what we speak, as we are each the owner of one of these *treasures:*

Mrs. R. W. Snow,	Mrs. Noah Kelsey,	Mrs. M. E. Root,
Mrs. E. S. Morse,	Mrs. Jonathan Hunt,	Mrs. C. C. Wheeler,
Mrs. E. P. Flint,	Mrs. Israel Knox,	Miss Sallie Snell,
Mrs. T. A. Mitchel,	Mrs. W. F. Kelsey,	Mrs. C. R. Allen,
Mrs. Elizabeth Hinckley,	Mrs. J. F. Cooke,	Miss Carrie Root,
Mrs. Dr. Carpenter,	Mrs. G. F. Alexander,	Mrs. W. C. Little,
Mrs. Dr. Knox,	Mrs. Marwedel,	Mrs. Duncan,
Mrs. Tilley,	Mrs. C. B. Parcells,	Mrs. Chas. Kellogg,
Miss Emma Garlie,	Mrs. Herrick,	Mrs. Niswander.

☞ Send for Descriptive Circular and Price List.

WILLCOX & GIBBS S. M. CO.
124 Post Street, San Francisco.

The wife and daughter of a prominent citizen assures us they feel that they cannot do without Kalliodont.

ALAMEDA COUNTY BRANCH

Solid Indemnity. Moderate Rates.   **Prompt and Liberal Statements.**

OF CALIFORNIA.
924 BROADWAY, OAKLAND.

Capital, paid up	$3,000,000 00
Assets, January 1, 1883	717,156 63
Surplus for Policy-Holders	710,860 63
Income, 1882	312,349 02
Net Surplus	237,962 13

Largest Net Surplus of any California Company.

R. H. MAGILL, General Agent.

H. B. HOUGHTON, Secretary.   H. F. GORDON, Manager.

McCLEVERTY & NOBLETT,
FASHION

LIVERY AND   **SALE STABLE**

East Side of Broadway, Three Doors above R. R. Depot, Oakland.

Families supplied with HORSES, BUGGIES and LADIES' PHÆTONS on the most reasonable terms. HACKS, LAUDAULETTS, COUPLETTS or CABS can be found on the arrival of all Trains.

All Orders prompty attended to.

The Only Stable in Connection with District Telegraph and Telephone Co.

GALINDO HOTEL CARRIAGES.

CABS and HACKS at all Hours.   Nos. of HACKS---1, 2, 3, 4, 5 and 6.

www.ingramcontent.com/pod-product-compliance
Lightning Source LLC
Chambersburg PA
CBHW030355170426
43202CB00010B/1384